HOW TO
CAKE IT

HOW TO
CAKE IT

A Cakebook

Yolanda Gampp
Photography by Jeremy Kohm

Collins
An Imprint of HarperCollinsPublishersLtd

HOW TO CAKE IT

Published by Collins, an imprint of HarperCollins Publishers Ltd

First Canadian edition

Printed in the United States of America

Creative direction by Connie Contardi, Yolanda Gampp, and Jocelyn Mercer

Designed by Gareth Lind

Photography by Jeremy Kohm (with the exception of the photos on
pages 93 [nachos] and 94–97)

All illustrations from iStock.com, with the exception of Lucky Cat (Shutterstock)
and Sir Squeeze and Marquee Letter (Gareth Lind)

Library and Archives Canada Cataloguing in Publication information is available
upon request.

ISBN 978-1-44345-389-9

17 18 19 20 21   QGT   10 9 8 7 6 5 4 3 2 1

I dedicate this book to

my son, who I love every day,

my husband, who stands by my side every day,

and my father, who I miss every day.

| Yo's Italian Meringue Buttercream 30 | Yo's Chocolate Swiss Meringue Buttercream 32 | Yo's Simple Syrup 34 | Yo's Dark Chocolate Ganache 36 | Yo's Royal Icing 38 | Yo's Modeling Chocolate 40 |

| How to Crumb Coat and Chill 56 | How to Color Buttercream 58 | Don't Fear the Fondant 60 | How to Color Fondant 62 | How to Prepare and Roll Fondant 64 |

 Party Hat 103

 Giant Cake Slice 111

 Watermelon 121

 Golden Pyramid 171

 Mega Chocolate Bar 179

 Purse 189

 Toy Bulldozer 249

 Crown 261

 Lucky Cat 275

Here's everything you need to get baking and caking!

My Love Letter to Cake

You just never know where your dreams will take you.

I always believed that if I worked hard at my craft and practiced often, it would pay off—even if I didn't understand how. I've spent upwards of 30,000 hours alone in my kitchen making cakes, and in all that time I could *never* have predicted that *How To Cake It* would resonate with so many people or that someday millions of viewers and subscribers would be watching me do what I love and be inspired to try it themselves. It blows my mind. When people leave comments asking "Is that *really* cake!?" my heart smiles.

I've been baking from a young age, inspired by my father, who was also a baker as well as my hero. I have his handwritten banana muffin recipe framed in my kitchen, and still use his serrated knife to level and carve my cakes—it's older than I am! After attending culinary school, I knew that being a chef was not for me; baking

was where I wanted to focus. So I went out and got a job in a large commercial bakery that made classic iced cakes and goodies, and I began to learn the basics. At one point I was icing 120 cakes a day!

But then something happened: a woman came into the bakery with a magazine that had a picture of an incredible cake decorated with something called fondant. I was fascinated—it was like combining baking and art! I managed to find a few books about novelty cakes, and as I flipped through them I became completely inspired and determined to figure out *how—how* do they cake it?

I started to experiment on my own whenever I could, making cakes for anyone who would take them. I took risks and tried new things, and never, ever gave up. Hours and weeks in my kitchen flew by, and eventually years. I left my job at the bakery so I could make novelty cakes full time, and my cakes started to get noticed. Writing my very own cakebook was always a dream that played in my mind. As I created

cake after cake after cake, I would imagine what my cakebook would look like, the types of cakes I would include, and how it would feel to see it on the shelves among all the other baking books I adore. I knew I had it in me, but how could I make it happen?

In the fall of 2014, I found myself at a major crossroads. My son was just a year old, and I was focused on the entirely new and exciting role of being a mother. I truly did not know what was next for me as a cake artist. Two big opportunities hadn't turned out the way I'd hoped: a television show called *SugarStars* I'd been cast in was cancelled, and I'd also been forced to let go of a business I started creating novelty cakes and sweet tables for events. I had poured my heart into that business. But as they say, when one chapter ends, another begins…

One day, Connie and Jocelyn, who were the creators of *SugarStars* and also good friends, called me up to find out if I'd be interested in starting a YouTube channel focused on my cakes. It would be a risk, with a lot of work and no guarantee of any success. "What

do I have to lose?" I thought. Off we went. *How To Cake It* allowed me to create the cakes I'd always dreamed of, and allowed Connie and Jocelyn to create content they truly believed in. To our amazement, the channel has blossomed into a global community of over six million cake enthusiasts (and growing!). It embodies three things that are very important to all three of us: collaboration, creativity, and consistency. Collaboration between three women, each with her own passion; creativity in how we share those passions with the world; and consistency in believing in ourselves and each other.

This book reflects my own experience going from a beginner baker to a cake artist, and it's designed to be something you can grow with whether you are just starting out or already a skilled caker. It builds core skills and confidence through detailed recipes and tips, but also contains hundreds of photos that I hope evoke possibilities, excitement, and inspiration. (My own mind works visually, so I have always gravitated toward studying the pictures in books more than reading the instructions.) I put my heart and soul into every single cake in this book, and it's been the hardest but most rewarding project I've done yet. And I'm very sentimental, so you may notice that I've tried to weave some of the people who mean the most to me into a few recipes.

We begin with the "Bake It" section and "Yo's Recipe Box," where I lay out all the recipes you'll need to build the cakes in this book. They have been crafted specifically for novelty caking, so follow them closely and do not worry if you don't get them right on the first go. Remember what I said above: practice often and it pays off! Next up, in "Yo Knows" I share my tips, tricks, and fundamental skills for success in caking.

Then the real fun starts! In the "Cake It" section I teach you how to create novelty cakes that will blow your friends and family away. If you are a beginner, start with "Caking Your First Steps," then build to "Cake It Up a Notch" and finish off with "Cake It to the Limit." Along the way you'll learn how to work with fondant, how to carve, how to perfect your crumb coat, and, most important, how to have fun doing it! My deepest hope is that you will make every cake your own—allow your imagination to run wild. To my amazing YoYos: I thank every single one of you for your comments, love, and encouragement. You are the reason *How To Cake It*—both the channel and the book—is possible. Many of you have told me that I make a positive impact on your life. Your words humble me, but I need you to know: you, too, have a positive impact on my life in ways I can't explain.

And to those of you who are new to the community—welcome! I hope you'll share the amazing cakes you create with me, and that you enjoy *How To Cake It* as much as we enjoy making it.

As you cake your way through this book, remember that creativity is all about believing in yourself and taking risks. If I hadn't done that, I wouldn't be here.

Love,
Yo xo

Ingredients

Cocoa powder

I use Dutch-processed for the deepest flavor

Confectioners' sugar

All-purpose flour

The perfect bed for rolling out my fondant so it doesn't stick

← **Baking soda**

← **Baking powder**

Grenadian vanilla

I only use vanilla from Grenada, my mom's home country

Tools

Rubber spatula →

Whisk

Wooden spoon ↙

Measuring cups and spoons ↙

Kitchen timer ↓

Don't forget to set it every time you bake!

Whip it good

↙ **Cake tester**

Wire rack ↙

Helps air to circulate underneath your cake as it cools

↙ **Candy thermometer**

A must-have for making my Italian Meringue Buttercream (page 30)

Parchment paper →

1 TBSP

1 TSP

1/2 TSP

1/4 TSP

Serrated knife →

This one was my dad's

1 2 3 4 5 6 7 8 9 10 11 12

Ruler ↑

My Bae! ♥♥♥
A must-have for leveling, layering, and measuring

Crucial for crumb coating

Bench scraper ↑

Straight and offset spatulas →

My main squeeze! Learn how to use him on page 52

Every cake artist needs a spatula collection! Different varieties work with different cakes and shapes

Sir Squeeze-A-Lot ↘

Small straight and offset spatulas ←

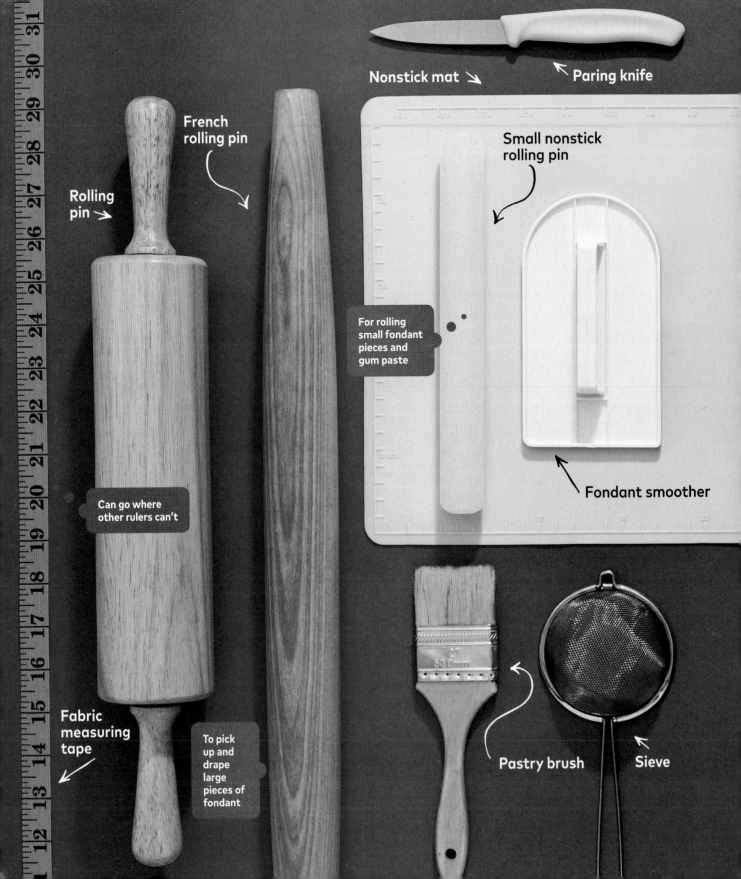

Paring knife

Nonstick mat

French rolling pin

Rolling pin

Small nonstick rolling pin

For rolling small fondant pieces and gum paste

Fondant smoother

Can go where other rulers can't

Fabric measuring tape

To pick up and drape large pieces of fondant

Pastry brush

Sieve

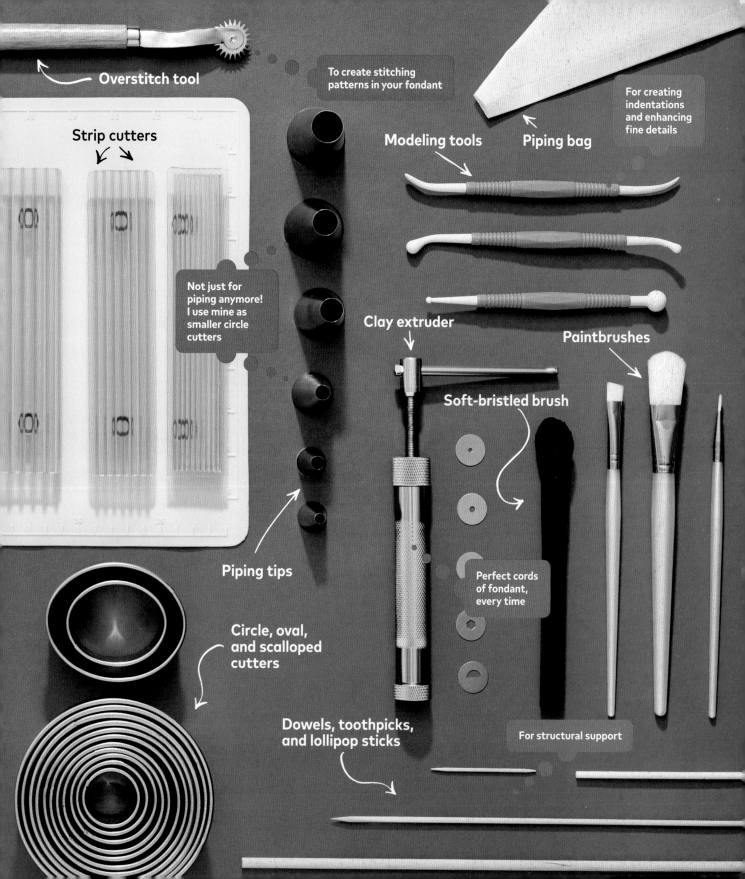

Overstitch tool

To create stitching patterns in your fondant

Strip cutters

Modeling tools

Piping bag

For creating indentations and enhancing fine details

Not just for piping anymore! I use mine as smaller circle cutters

Clay extruder

Paintbrushes

Soft-bristled brush

Piping tips

Circle, oval, and scalloped cutters

Perfect cords of fondant, every time

Dowels, toothpicks, and lollipop sticks

For structural support

Yo's Recipe Box

Welcome to my personal collection of tried, tested, and true baking essentials. From my Ultimate Vanilla Cake to my famous Italian Meringue Buttercream, you'll find all my can't-cake-without-it baking blueprints. I've been perfecting them for over 17 years, and I trust them to keep my cakes tasting as great as they look. Novelty cakes sometimes have a bad reputation. People will tell me that they've tried cake recipes that either weren't sturdy enough for carving or lacked flavor because they were too dense or too dry. But I've spent close to two decades perfecting these recipes to create moist, buttery, delicious cakes that firm up beautifully for carving when chilled. And of course, my sidekick Sir Squeeze-A-Lot and his magical simple syrup also help to seal in the moisture and flavor of your cakes, no matter how long they take to decorate.

Although these recipes are perfectly suited for all your novelty cake adventures, you can also turn to them for simple, everyday cakes that will help build your baking confidence and satisfy your sweet tooth.

Have fun baking, but make sure that you improvise on the decorating rather than on the recipes themselves. While caking is an art, baking is a science, and these recipes should be followed exactly. Now, time to roll up your sleeves, crank up your favorite kitchen playlist, and get baking!

Yo's Ultimate Chocolate Cake

This chocolate cake is my go-to recipe. It's moist and delicious, and also sturdy enough to carve into novelty cakes like the ones you see on *How To Cake It*. I've been making this chocolate cake recipe for 15 years, with a few tweaks here and there, and it has never let me down, whether it's smothered in buttercream, draped with fondant, or dripping with ganache.

If you're making one of the novelty cakes, use the pan sizes and baking times specified in the novelty cake recipe.

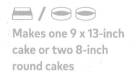

Makes one 9 x 13-inch cake or two 8-inch round cakes

Ingredients

2¾ cups	all-purpose flour
2 teaspoons	baking powder
1½ teaspoons	baking soda
1 teaspoon	table salt
1 cup	Dutch-processed cocoa powder
1 cup (2 sticks)	unsalted butter, at room temperature
2½ cups	sugar
4	large eggs, at room temperature

1 Preheat the oven to 350°F. Line the bottom of each cake pan with parchment paper (see "How to Bake a Cake" on page 44).

2 Sift the flour, baking powder, baking soda, and salt into a medium bowl and whisk together. Set aside.

3 Put the cocoa powder in a medium heatproof bowl. Bring 3 cups water to a boil, then carefully measure exactly 2 cups and pour over the cocoa powder and whisk until completely smooth. Set aside to cool slightly.

4 In the bowl of a stand mixer fitted with the paddle attachment, beat the butter and sugar on medium speed until light and fluffy, about 8 minutes.

5 Add the eggs, two at a time, beating until each addition is incorporated before adding the next. Scrape down the sides of the bowl with a spatula when necessary.

6 Add the flour mixture in four parts, alternating with the warm cocoa mixture in three parts, beating just until each addition is incorporated before adding the next; do not overmix.

7 Pour the batter into the prepared pan or pans. Bake until a toothpick inserted in the center comes out clean, about 45 minutes for the 9 × 13-inch pan or 55 minutes for the 8-inch pans, rotating the pan(s) halfway through.

8 Transfer to a wire rack and let cool completely in the pan(s). Cover tightly with plastic wrap and refrigerate overnight. Loosen the edges with a straight spatula, invert the pan(s) to remove the cake, and peel off the parchment.

Yo's Ultimate Vanilla Cake

I am really proud of this vanilla cake. I love its buttery, sweet flavor, and its texture is perfect for simple cakes layered with buttercream and toppings as well as for novelty cakes. It is subtle yet satisfying, and tastes homemade and much better than the artificial-vanilla boxed variety.

If you're making one of the novelty cakes, use the pan sizes and baking times specified in the novelty cake recipe.

Makes one 9 × 13-inch cake or two 8-inch round cakes

Fun things you can do with vanilla cake? Dye it with food coloring, or throw in sprinkles for a festive funfetti look!

Ingredients

2½ cups	all-purpose flour
2½ teaspoons	baking powder
½ teaspoon	table salt
1 cup (2 sticks)	unsalted butter, at room temperature
2 cups	sugar
1 teaspoon	pure vanilla extract
4	large eggs, at room temperature
1 cup	whole milk

1 Preheat the oven to 350°F. Line the bottom of each cake pan with parchment paper (see "How to Bake a Cake" on page 44).

2 Sift the flour, baking powder, and salt into a medium bowl and whisk together. Set aside.

3 In the bowl of a stand mixer fitted with the paddle attachment, beat the butter, sugar, and vanilla on medium speed until light and fluffy, about 8 minutes.

4 Add the eggs, two at a time, beating until each addition is incorporated before adding the next. Scrape down the sides of the bowl with a spatula when necessary.

5 Add the flour mixture in four parts, alternating with the milk in three parts, beating just until each addition is incorporated before adding the next; do not overmix.

6 Scrape the batter into the prepared pan or pans and spread it so that it is smooth in the pan(s). Bake until a toothpick inserted in the center comes out clean, about 40 minutes for the 9 × 13-inch pan or 45 minutes for the 8-inch pans, rotating the pan(s) halfway through.

7 Transfer to a wire rack and let cool completely in the pan(s). Cover tightly with plastic wrap and refrigerate overnight. Loosen the edges with a straight spatula, invert the pan(s) to remove the cake, and peel off the parchment.

Yo's Pink Velvet Cake

This bright and eye-catching cake is best known from my Watermelon Cake (page 121). Unlike traditional red velvet batter, this does not contain cocoa powder, which would overpower the pink food coloring.

But don't stop at pink. Experiment with all of the colors in the rainbow!

Makes one 9 × 13-inch cake or two 8-inch round cakes

> If you don't have buttermilk, stir 2 teaspoons cider vinegar or distilled white vinegar into 2 cups room-temperature whole milk and let stand for 10 to 15 minutes, until the milk has thickened slightly.

Ingredients

4 cups	all-purpose flour
2 teaspoons	table salt
1 cup (2 sticks)	unsalted butter, at room temperature
⅓ cup	vegetable oil
3 cups	sugar
1½ teaspoons	pure vanilla extract
	Gel food colorings: rose and red
4	large eggs, at room temperature
2 cups	buttermilk, at room temperature (see Tip)
2 teaspoons	baking soda
2 teaspoons	cider vinegar

1 Preheat the oven to 350°F. Line the bottom of each cake pan with parchment paper (see "How to Bake a Cake" on page 44).

2 Sift the flour and salt into a medium bowl and whisk together. Set aside.

3 In the bowl of a stand mixer fitted with the paddle attachment, beat the butter, oil, sugar, and vanilla on medium speed until well combined, about 5 minutes.

4 Add 1 tablespoon rose and ½ teaspoon red food coloring and beat until the batter is evenly colored. Scrape the sides and bottom of the bowl to make sure all the mixture is colored.

5 Add the eggs, two at a time, beating until each addition is incorporated before adding the next. Scrape down the sides of the bowl with a spatula when necessary.

6 Add the flour mixture in four parts, alternating with the buttermilk in three parts, beating just until each addition is incorporated before adding the next; do not overmix.

7 In a small cup, combine the baking soda and vinegar. With the mixer running, immediately add the mixture to the batter. Beat for 10 seconds.

8 Scrape the batter into the prepared pan or pans and spread it so that it is smooth in the pan(s). Bake until a toothpick inserted in the center comes out clean, about 45 minutes for the 9 × 13-inch pan or 55 minutes for the 8-inch pans, rotating the pan(s) halfway through.

9 Transfer to a wire rack and let cool completely in the pan(s). Cover tightly with plastic wrap and refrigerate overnight. Loosen the edges with a straight spatula, invert the pan(s) to remove the cake, and peel off the parchment.

Yo's Coconut Cake

I **'m a *big* coconut fan.** I am half Grenadian, so I think it's in my blood. I love the subtly sweet taste of coconut cake as well as its richness. This recipe uses both coconut milk and sweetened desiccated coconut for a double dose of flavor—no coconut extract needed. I'm crazy about it and I have managed to convert many coconut haters with this delicious cake.

If you're making one of the novelty cakes, use the pan sizes and baking times specified in the novelty cake recipe.

Makes one 9 × 13-inch cake or two 8-inch round cakes

Ingredients

3 cups	all-purpose flour
1 tablespoon	baking powder
1 cup	sweetened desiccated or shredded coconut
1 cup (2 sticks)	salted butter, at room temperature
2 cups	sugar
2 teaspoons	pure vanilla extract
4	large egg whites, at room temperature
4	large whole eggs, at room temperature
2⅓ cups	unsweetened coconut milk (a bit less than 1½ [13.5-ounce] cans)

1 Preheat the oven to 350°F. Line the bottom of each cake pan with parchment paper (see "How to Bake a Cake" on page 44).

2 Sift the flour and baking powder into a medium bowl, then whisk in the desiccated coconut. Set aside.

3 In the bowl of a stand mixer fitted with the paddle attachment, beat the butter, sugar, and vanilla on medium speed until light and fluffy, about 8 minutes.

4 Add the egg whites and whole eggs, two at a time, beating until each addition is incorporated before adding the next. Scrape down the sides of the bowl with a spatula when necessary.

5 Add the flour mixture in four parts, alternating with the coconut milk in three parts, beating just until each addition is incorporated before adding the next; do not overmix.

6 Scrape the batter into the prepared pan or pans and spread it so that it is smooth in the pan(s). Bake until a toothpick inserted in the center comes out clean, about 45 minutes for the 9 × 13-inch pan or 55 minutes for the 8-inch pans, rotating the pan(s) halfway through.

7 Transfer to a wire rack and let cool completely in the pan(s). Cover tightly with plastic wrap and refrigerate overnight. Loosen the edges with a straight spatula, invert the pan(s) to remove the cake, and peel off the parchment.

Yo's Italian Meringue Buttercream

Makes about 6 cups

I **make this buttercream** by the boatload. One of the things I love about Italian meringue buttercream is that it goes on so smoothly, providing the perfect surface for fondant. And for flavor, you just can't beat this buttercream: it's light yet creamy and not too sweet, as American buttercream or other types of frosting can be, because it doesn't rely on icing sugar.

If you're working with frozen buttercream, let it thaw overnight in the fridge and then sit at room temperature for 2 to 4 hours. If you can't wait that long, you can place your fresh-from-the-fridge buttercream in the bowl of a stand mixer fitted with a whisk attachment, wrap a hot towel around the bowl, and whip at high speed until it reaches room temperature.

Ingredients

1¾ cups	sugar
8	large egg whites, at room temperature
2 cups (4 sticks)	unsalted butter, cut into tablespoon-size pieces, at room temperature
1 teaspoon	pure vanilla extract

1 In a small saucepan, combine the sugar and ½ cup water. Place over medium heat and bring to a boil. Clip a candy thermometer to the side of the pan.

2 While the sugar syrup is heating, put the egg whites in the bowl of a stand mixer fitted with the whisk attachment.

3 When the syrup reaches 230°F on the candy thermometer, begin to whip the egg whites on medium-high speed. Whip until the egg whites are stiff.

4 When the syrup reaches 240°F, immediately remove the pan from the heat and, with the mixer running, pour the syrup into the egg whites in a very thin stream. Pour the syrup between the side of the bowl and the whisk attachment.

5 Whip the meringue at high speed until thick and glossy and the bowl is no longer warm on the outside, about 8 to 12 minutes.

6 With the mixer running, add the butter, a piece at a time, whipping until each piece is fully incorporated before adding the next. Scrape down the sides of the bowl with a spatula occasionally.

7 After all the butter has been added, continue to whip the buttercream until it's thick and smooth, 3 to 5 minutes. Beat in the vanilla.

8 Use immediately or transfer to an airtight container and store in the refrigerator for up to 1 week or the freezer for up to 2 months. Before using refrigerated or frozen buttercream, let it warm up to room temperature and stir to smooth it out.

Yo's Chocolate Swiss Meringue Buttercream

I **personally love this** buttercream because it's as light and smooth as Italian meringue buttercream but delightfully chocolaty. It isn't too rich, so it pairs perfectly with any cake, satisfying chocolate cravings without overpowering other flavors. If you've got a young chocoholic in your house, this is *the* buttercream to use on all your cakes!

This buttercream needs a bit of time to set up—there's *a lot* of chocolate. Make it at least a day ahead.

Makes about 6 cups

Ingredients

18 ounces	good-quality dark chocolate
1 cup	sugar
¼ teaspoon	table salt
⅛ teaspoon	cream of tartar
4	large egg whites
2 cups (4 sticks)	unsalted butter, cut into tablespoon size pieces, at room temperature

1 Chop the chocolate as finely as you can. Put it in a heatproof bowl and set the bowl over a pan of lightly simmering water (do not let the bowl touch the water).

2 Melt the chocolate, stirring until smooth, then remove the bowl from the saucepan and set aside to cool while you prepare the buttercream. Leave the pan of water on the stove, as you will need it shortly.

3 In the bowl of a stand mixer, whisk together the sugar, salt, and cream of tartar. Whisk in the egg whites until thoroughly combined.

4 Place the bowl with the egg whites over the pan of simmering water (again, do not let the bowl touch the water). Heat the mixture, whisking frequently, until it's warm but not hot to the touch and the sugar is mostly dissolved (you should feel just a little grittiness when you rub a bit of the mixture between your fingertips), about 2 to 5 minutes.

5 Transfer the bowl to the stand mixer and fit the mixer with the whisk attachment. Whip at high speed until thick and glossy and the bowl is no longer warm on the outside, about 5 minutes.

6 With the mixer running, add the butter, a piece at a time, whipping until each piece is fully incorporated before adding the next. Scrape down the sides of the bowl with a spatula occasionally.

7 After all the butter has been added, continue to whip the buttercream until it's thick and smooth, 3 to 5 minutes.

8 Check the melted chocolate: It should be soft and liquid, not firm; if it's completely cooled and thickened, set the bowl over the still-hot water in the saucepan for just a few seconds and stir until it's soft but not warm. Scrape the chocolate into the buttercream and whip on high speed until fully incorporated.

9 Keep in a cool, dry place for up to a day. If you're making this more than a day in advance, transfer to an airtight container and store in the refrigerator for up to 1 week or the freezer for up to 1 month. Before using refrigerated or frozen buttercream, let it warm up to room temperature and stir to smooth it out.

Yo's Simple Syrup

If you've seen just *one* episode of *How To Cake It*, you've seen me use simple syrup—and Sir Squeeze-A-Lot, my magical simple syrup squeeze bottle. (Try saying that five times fast!) I sprinkle this magical mixture on every single one of my cakes to keep them moist throughout assembly, decoration, and refrigeration. This is especially important when you're making complex novelty cakes, as they often take several days to carve, cover with fondant, and decorate. See page 52 for details about how to use simple syrup.

Makes about 1½ cups

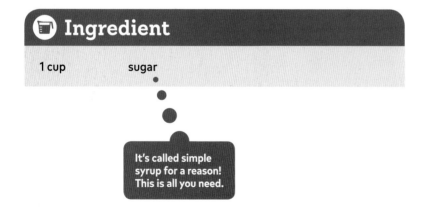

Ingredient

1 cup	sugar

It's called simple syrup for a reason! This is all you need.

1 In a small saucepan, combine the sugar and 1 cup water and bring to a boil over medium heat, stirring until the sugar is completely dissolved.

2 Let cool completely, then cover and store in the refrigerator for up to 1 month.

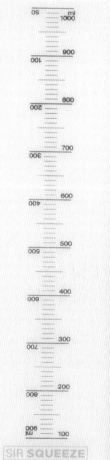

Yo's Dark Chocolate Ganache

Ganache is one of my favorite ways to incorporate chocolate into a cake. You can drizzle it, dip cupcakes in it, pipe it, and even crumb coat with it! It's simple, rich, and an instant crowd-pleaser—and about as close to pure melted chocolate as you can get.

This proportion of chocolate to cream (1:1 by weight) makes a pourable ganache that firms up to a creamy-smooth spreadable consistency when cool.

Makes 3 cups

> To make white chocolate ganache, simply substitute 2 pounds white chocolate for 1 pound of the dark.

Ingredients

I use between 56% and 72%.

1 pound	good-quality dark chocolate
2 cups	whipping cream

1 Chop the chocolate as finely as you can. Place it in a heatproof bowl.

2 Pour the cream into a heavy saucepan and place over medium-high heat. Bring just to a simmer—you should see bubbles around the edges of the pot and movement just under the surface of the cream. Do not let it boil.

3. Pour the hot cream over the chocolate and cover the bowl with a lid or plastic wrap. Let stand for 10 to 15 minutes.

4. Uncover the bowl and gently stir with a spatula, starting in the middle and working your way out. The ganache will start to darken and come together into a velvety mixture. To ensure that no lumps are left, pour the ganache through a sieve into a clean bowl.

5. Use the ganache right away for drizzling or dipping, or let it cool for at least several hours or overnight if you're spreading it as icing.

6. If you won't be using the ganache within a day, transfer it to an airtight container and store in the refrigerator for up to 1 week or the freezer for up to 2 months. Before using refrigerated or frozen ganache, let it warm up to room temperature.

> If the ganache becomes too firm to spread as you're working with it, gently reheat it in the microwave for no more than 10 seconds at a time until spreadable, stirring in between.

Yo's Royal Icing

Makes about 1¼ cups

I consider royal icing my cake super glue—it just helps everything stick together! When water or piping gel won't cut it, royal icing is the sturdiest of edible glues. I always have a container of it kicking around in the fridge. It's perfect for attaching fondant details, hiding flaws, patching, and covering up fondant seams on white cakes. And it's incredibly easy to make—just two ingredients and a little time in the stand mixer. Best of all? While it sticks like crazy to cake, it won't stick your fingers together, unlike regular super glue!

Ingredients

2½ tablespoons	meringue powder
1¾ cups	confectioners' sugar

1. In a medium bowl, whisk together the meringue powder and 3 tablespoons water until foamy.

2. Add the confectioners' sugar and beat with a handheld electric mixer at low speed until very thick and smooth, 3 to 5 minutes. Turn the mixer up to medium speed and beat for 1 minute.

3 If your icing is too runny, stiffen it by adding more confectioners' sugar; if it's too thick, stir in a little more water.

4 Cover the bowl with a damp cloth until you're ready to use the icing.

5 If you're making this more than a few hours in advance, transfer to an airtight container and press a sheet of plastic wrap directly on the surface to prevent a crust from forming, then store in the refrigerator. The icing will keep for up to 1 month in the fridge.

Royal icing can be tinted with food colorings: Add just a little at a time, stirring to incorporate each addition until you have the color you want.

Yo's Modeling Chocolate

Modeling chocolate is one of the most versatile tools in my caking toolkit. You can dye it, sculpt fine details with it, mold it, run it through a pasta machine, even grate it if you're in need of some modeling chocolate "cheese." The only trick to this recipe is that you need to be sure to make the chocolate in advance—it needs to sit for a day before you can work with it. Don't be fooled and think that you can substitute white chocolate chips for compound chocolate—you won't get the same smooth, workable consistency.

Makes a little over 1 pound

You can also make dark modeling chocolate. Just substitute dark compound chocolate for the white, and use either light or regular corn syrup.

Ingredients

12 ounces	white chocolate compound chocolate
½ cup	light corn syrup
	Gel food colorings (optional; as specified in the cake recipes)

1 Put the compound chocolate and corn syrup in a heatproof bowl and set the bowl over a pan of lightly simmering water (do not let the bowl touch the water).

2 Let the chocolate melt a bit, then stir gently with a spatula to combine the ingredients. Stir until smooth and homogenous.

3 If you're coloring the modeling chocolate different colors, transfer it to separate bowls and stir in food colorings before the chocolate cools.

4 Let cool to room temperature, then cover the bowls with plastic wrap and let stand at room temperature overnight.

Bake It

Yo Knows

If **knowledge is power,** then this next section is going to make you a caking superhero! These are my core caking practices—all the novelty cake techniques and processes that I've spent A LOT of time learning myself. From simple syruping to crumb coating and chilling, these primary caking skills will serve as the foundation for your caking future. I use these techniques and processes in just about every single novelty cake presented in this book and on my YouTube channel, so they are the perfect first steps to getting comfortable with any caking project.

Caking is both an art and a craft. The art of it invites you to be creative and experimental and to just have fun with it, while the craft of caking asks you to practice the basics. I learned everything I know about novelty caking through books and practice, so I'm really excited you're on the same path. But even after all these years, I remain hungry to learn more. I hope you feel the same and will continue to refer to this book as your guide. Just remember to stick with it. Practice these techniques and soon you'll know as much as I do—and who knows where that could lead!

How to Bake a Cake

What You'll Need

Cake pan (3 inches deep) or sphere cake pan

Parchment paper

Pencil

Scissors

Vegetable shortening

Cake batter (pages 22–29)

Rubber spatula

Paring knife or straight spatula

Timer

Cake tester or toothpick

Wire rack

Don't be shallow! Cake pans need to be 3 inches deep.

1 Preheat the oven to 350°F. Place your cake pan on a sheet of parchment paper, and with a pencil, trace its outline. Cut the parchment to size with scissors and use it to line the bottom of the pan, spreading small bits of shortening on the bottom of the pan to secure it.

2 Scrape the batter into the prepared pan with the help of a rubber spatula—you don't want to leave any yummy batter behind!

3 To line a sphere cake pan with parchment, cut a round piece of parchment that is 2 inches wider than the diameter of the sphere pan. If you have a cake pan of that size, you can trace around that. Fold the circle in half and then into a quarter. With scissors, cut slits along the fold lines from the outside edge to halfway to the center, then cut three to five slits the same length in between (like you're cutting a pie). This way, the parchment will fit the curves of the pan without wrinkling. Use shortening to stick the parchment to the pan. Allow your slits to naturally overlap. If there is any exposed cake pan above your parchment, be sure to grease that well with shortening.

4 If the batter is thick (like my vanilla cake batter) and doesn't naturally spread flat, smooth the top with a rubber spatula, making sure to fill the corners of the pan.

5 To remove any air bubbles in the batter, run a paring knife or a straight spatula through the batter in a grid pattern, first going horizontally and then vertically. Give the pan a few good taps on your work surface to release any remaining air bubbles.

For some of these cakes, you'll have to bake in batches, and rearrange your oven racks to accommodate the pans. If you have a conventional oven, aim to bake the cakes on the center rack.

6 Set a timer for half the recommended baking time. When the timer goes off, rotate your cake pan 180 degrees. Reset the timer to 5 to 10 minutes less than the remaining baking time. Baking times are always suggestions, and all ovens are different, so it's always helpful to keep a close eye on your cakes as they bake.

I prefer pans with straight sides.

7 Check the cake for doneness: Insert a cake tester or toothpick into the center of the cake and remove it. If batter or wet crumbs are stuck to the tester, continue to bake in 10-minute increments, then check again. When the cake is done, the cake tester or toothpick will come out clean.

8 Transfer the cake to a wire rack and let cool completely in the pan, then cover the pan tightly with plastic wrap and refrigerate overnight. (This helps firm up the cake so it keeps its shape.)

9 To remove the cake from the pan, loosen the edges with a straight spatula, holding the flat part of the blade flush with the side of the pan, and pulling along all sides. Invert the cake onto a cake board or work surface, and peel off the parchment.

CAKÉ

How to Level and Layer a Cake

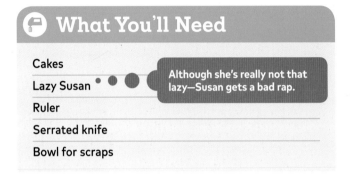

🖐 What You'll Need

Cakes

Lazy Susan

Although she's really not that lazy—Susan gets a bad rap.

Ruler

Serrated knife

Bowl for scraps

got cake?

1 Remove the cakes from the pans and peel off the parchment. Place one cake right side up on a lazy Susan. Because the cake may not be an even height, it's important to identify the shortest side of the cake. Hold a ruler upright and flush against the shortest side of the cake and make a mark with a serrated knife just before the rounded top starts. Continue to move the ruler incrementally around the cake, marking the same measurement with the serrated knife all the way around. Place your hand on top of the cake dome and apply gentle pressure to slowly turn the lazy Susan. Begin to join the marks with the serrated knife, making a shallow, continuous cut around the cake.

2 Continue to rotate the cake while you cut a little deeper all the way around until the knife reaches the center. This is the best way to ensure a clean and even cut.

I like to use a long serrated knife so I can always see the knife on both sides of the cake. This way I can be sure I'm not digging down into the center of the cake with the tip of my knife and creating a valley.

Cake scraps are delicious—we often get into cake scrap scraps!

3 Lift off the dome and put it in the bowl.

4 Turn your leveled cake upside down and remove the thin layer of caramelization (the browned part) from the bottom using the same technique as you did with the leveling. I usually remove ⅛ to ¼ inch of caramelization. Add those to the scrap bowl, too.

5 To split the cake into two layers, use the ruler to find the midpoint of the side of the cake and mark it incrementally around the cake with the knife. Using the same technique that you used to level the cake, cut the cake in half.

YO
KNOWS

How to Simple Syrup a Cake

What You'll Need

Sir Squeeze-A-Lot bottle ● ● ● **Unicorn sweater optional. #ootd**

Funnel

Yo's Simple Syrup (page 34) in a liquid measuring cup

Cake layers

1 Take the nozzle top off the Sir Squeeze-A-Lot bottle and insert the funnel. Slowly pour the simple syrup through the funnel into the bottle. Remove the funnel and replace the nozzle top. To prevent leaking, make sure you screw on the nozzle all the way, then press it down securely.

2 Hold the bottle upside down, keeping it straight, and use both hands to shower syrup onto your cake layers. Start with the outer edges and work into the center of each layer. Make sure not to oversaturate your cakes with syrup.

3 Let the syrup soak in for 5 to 10 minutes, then proceed with filling and layering. If the syrup hasn't fully soaked in, it'll make it more difficult to spread your desired filling, so make sure to give it enough time.

If you don't have a Sir Squeeze-A-Lot bottle (they're available at howtocakeit.com), pour the simple syrup into a small bowl and brush onto the cake layers using a pastry brush. Be careful when using a natural-bristle pastry brush, as the bristles can shed onto the cake. (This is why I prefer to use Sir Squeeze.)

How to Fill a Cake

What You'll Need

Cake layers soaked with simple syrup (see page 52)

Lazy Susan

Rubber spatula

Buttercream (page 30 or 32) in a bowl

Large offset spatula

1 Place the first cake layer on the lazy Susan. Using a rubber spatula, place a big dollop of buttercream in the center of the cake layer.

If the bottom of your spatula comes into contact with your cake it will begin to dredge up crumbs, making your buttercream very messy (and you know I don't like a mess). So try not to let this happen.

2 Using an offset spatula, start to spread the mound of buttercream over the cake layer, being careful not to scrape the surface of the cake with the spatula. Slowly turn the lazy Susan to help make covering the entire top easier. Spread the buttercream just a bit over the edges. If your layer of buttercream is too thin, add another small dollop and spread.

3 When the surface of your first cake layer is entirely covered with an even layer of buttercream, set the next cake layer on top and cover it with buttercream the same way.

4 Repeat until you've filled and stacked all the cake layers. Place the final cake layer on top, but don't cover it with buttercream.

How to Crumb Coat and Chill

🄵 What You'll Need

Filled cake (see page 54)

Lazy Susan

Spatulas: straight, rubber, and offset

Buttercream (page 30 or 32) in a bowl

Small bowl for scraping crumbs

This step is worth dancing for! It will ensure that no crumbs will show up in your buttercream when you ice your cake.

Give the lazy Susan a spin—you know, just for fun!

1 Place the cake on the lazy Susan. You'll have a bit of buttercream peeking out from between the cake layers. Press a straight spatula almost flat against the side of the cake and hold it steady while you slowly turn the lazy Susan to spread that buttercream evenly around the cake.

Hold the spatula firmly as you're working your way around the cake, spinning the lazy Susan to match your movement as you go.

2 Use a rubber spatula to add a big dollop of buttercream to the top of your cake. Use a straight or offset spatula to move a small portion of that buttercream to the side of the cake. Spread a thin layer of buttercream all the way around the cake, pressing the crumbs into the cake as you go, and taking more buttercream from the dollop as needed.

3 Scrape any crumb-y buttercream into the spare bowl as you go. You don't want any crumbs contaminating your gorgeous bowl of untouched buttercream.

4 When the cake sides are covered, spread the dollop of buttercream on the top of the cake. Use your spatula to go around the sides of your cake once again, smoothing any excess buttercream.

5 You'll notice a bit of excess buttercream around the top edge of the cake. Pull the buttercream into the center of the cake with your offset spatula, keeping the spatula flat on the top of your cake so that the top of your cake is covered with a thin layer and the edges are as sharp as possible. Chill for 20 to 30 minutes, until the buttercream layer is firm to the touch.

How to Color Buttercream

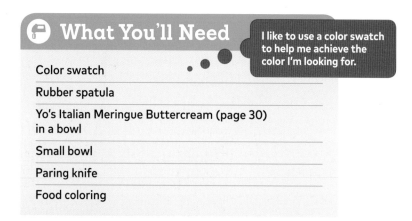

🅕 What You'll Need

I like to use a color swatch to help me achieve the color I'm looking for.

Color swatch

Rubber spatula

Yo's Italian Meringue Buttercream (page 30) in a bowl

Small bowl

Paring knife

Food coloring

That's why it's important to test in a smaller bowl first!

1 With a rubber spatula, scoop a test portion of buttercream into a small bowl. Add some food coloring using the tip of a paring knife or a drop straight from the bottle—keep note of how much you add. Stir it in until the buttercream is evenly colored and compare the color of the buttercream to the color swatch. If the color is too light, stir in more food coloring; if it's too dark, stir in more uncolored buttercream to dilute the color.

2 When you're happy with the color of the test portion, try to recreate that same color with the remaining buttercream. Add coloring a little at a time and stir until the color is thoroughly blended in, making sure to scrape the sides and bottom of your bowl.

3 Add the test portion of the buttercream into your large bowl and compare the color of the buttercream to the color swatch. Add more food coloring if needed.

It's important to test your color in a smaller bowl first because it allows you determine if you've chosen the right food coloring for your desired hue. At this point you may want to switch coloring or combine colors to get things just right.

Don't Fear the Fondant

I love working with fondant. As a cake-decorating medium, nothing compares. It can be shaped, texturized, smoothed—and of course it's edible, too.

When I first started caking, I worked in a bakery where they made all kinds of cake except for fondant cakes. I experimented with lots of different decorating materials and techniques, from piping to modeling chocolate, but I still felt limited. Then one day, I saw a photo of a fondant cake that inspired me to give that sugary magic a try. It was pretty much love at first knead! As soon as I started to work with fondant, my life as a cake artist changed forever. My caking possibilities now seemed endless.

Many of my YoYos tell me that they find fondant intimidating, but I'm here to assure you that there's no need to fear it. Fondant is your friend. You just need to get to know him a little better!

What Is Fondant?

Fondant is a moldable, rollable, edible paste made of sugars and starches. You can buy it premade at many grocery stores and craft shops or online, or you can make it yourself.

Find Your Fondant

When it comes to picking a fondant brand or recipe, there is no right or wrong. Test out different fondants to find the one that feels just right for you.

Climate Change

Fondant reacts to its environment. It can get sweaty on a humid day, or dry on a cold one, so pay attention to how your fondant reacts to your environment and adjust accordingly. If your fondant gets dry from the cold, you can soften it by kneading in a little vegetable shortening. If your fondant sweats in the heat, don't sweat it—it will eventually stop. Just try not to play with it too much in the meantime.

All You Knead…

One of the greatest things about fondant is that it's flexible, so you can change its state by kneading other things into it. For example, if your fondant is too soft, knead in a little CMC powder to strengthen it.

In Living Color

You can change the color of your fondant by kneading in food coloring (see page 62), or you can buy pre-colored fondant. Working with colored fondant can stain your hands and work surface. Adding a lot of color can also change the consistency of the fondant, so you'll want to give it time to settle. For shades that require you to add a lot of color, you may also need to add CMC powder to give the fondant strength and elasticity. It's a good idea to color a little more fondant than you think you'll need so that you don't run out and have to color match a new batch mid-way through caking.

Waste Not

If stored properly, fondant has a long shelf life, so there's no need to toss leftovers. Simply knead any excess into a ball, wrap it tightly in plastic wrap, and store in an airtight container in a cool, dry place.

What's Old Is New

If you have leftover fondant in specific colors—like Thanksgiving turkey brown—why not experiment with mixing colors together to create new ones? For example, mixing that turkey brown with some black food coloring will create black fondant.

Patch Work

When you're covering spherical cakes or cakes that taper in at the bottom, you may get a lot of creasing and folds. Fear not—you can fill those folds and creases, as well as any cracks, by turning your fondant into a paste. First, try your best to cut away any excess, then mix the extra fondant with water to form a paste that has a consistency like royal icing. Chill your cake, then use the fondant paste as a putty to fill the remaining creases. Check out how I created and used fondant paste on my Piggy Bank cake (page 151; step 14).

Handle with Care

When working with fondant, try to be light-handed. Don't be afraid to handle it, but practice being gentle with it, as fingerprints and long nails will indent the fondant if you're not careful. As with all things caking, practice is the key here!

Cake Protection

Sir Squeeze-A-Lot and fondant work together to keep your cakes moist. Sir Squeeze showers your cakes with simple syrup, infusing them with moisture, and the fondant acts as a protective layer that keeps that moisture locked in. Because of this, fondant-covered cakes last longer and taste fresher—as long as you haven't sliced them!

Flavor Profile

Some people love the taste of fondant and others find it too sweet. If you're not a fan of fondant, no problem! It's very easy to peel it away from a slice of cake, leaving you with the moist cake and delicious buttercream inside.

How to Color Fondant

What You'll Need

Color swatch

Vegetable shortening 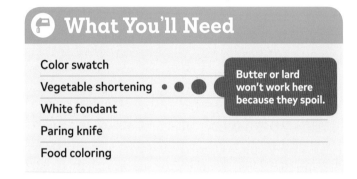 **Butter or lard won't work here because they spoil.**

White fondant

Paring knife

Food coloring

> When matching a specific color, such as apple green, I like to use a color swatch or the real thing as a model.

1 Rub a small amount of shortening on your hands. This will help prevent the fondant from sticking to your hands when you knead it. Use a paring knife to cut off a small test portion of fondant. It's important to test your color with a smaller piece of fondant because it allows you to determine if you've chosen the right food coloring for your desired hue. At this point you may want to switch coloring or combine colors for the perfect match.

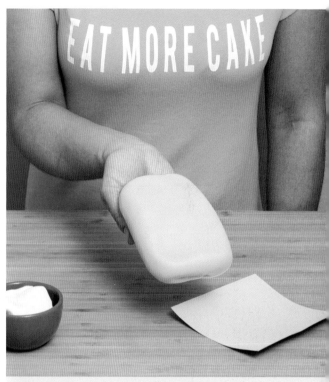

2 Fold the fondant over itself and keep folding and kneading until the color is evenly blended.

3 When you're happy with the color of the test portion, try to recreate that same color with the remaining fondant. Add your color a little at a time and knead until the color is thoroughly blended in. Hold the colored fondant against the color swatch. If the color is too dark, fold in more white fondant; if it's too light, fold in more food coloring.

How to Prepare and Roll Fondant

What You'll Need

Vegetable shortening	Wooden rolling pin
Fondant	Pastry brush
Fabric measuring tape	Plastic scraper
Sieve	Straight pin
Confectioners' sugar	

1 Rub a little vegetable shortening on your hands. Knead the fondant well using your palms—this helps to soften it and release air bubbles.

2 Begin to shape the fondant into a ball, tucking the seams to the underside as you go. The top of your ball should be completely smooth.

3 Press and squeeze the ball of fondant into a flat disk so it will be easier to roll out.

4 Before you roll your fondant, use a fabric measuring tape to measure your cake or the area you need to cover.

How to Prepare and Roll Fondant

6 While you're rolling, check with the measuring tape to ensure the fondant is big enough. I usually roll my fondant ⅛ inch thick to cover a cake. Don't worry if you can't get your fondant this thin on your first try! Some details require a different thickness, and some cakes (like the Jumbo Candy Apple, page 133) look better with a thinner covering of fondant.

5 Using a sieve, dust your work surface with confectioners' sugar and lay your disk of fondant on it. Using your rolling pin, roll from the center, and make sure to roll in every direction—away from you and toward you, side to side, and diagonally, keeping the shape of your cake in mind. For example, if your cake is round, you'll want to roll out the fondant into a circular shape.

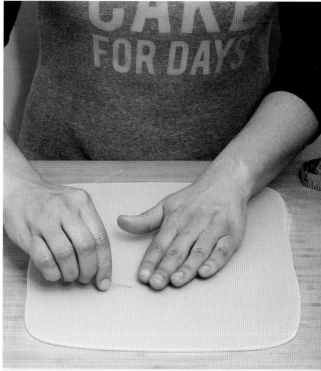

7 As you roll, brush away any confectioners' sugar that has ended up on the surface of your fondant. Use your scraper to remove excess confectioners' sugar that has gathered around the edges of the fondant (so the fondant sticks to the buttercream better). As the sheet gets bigger, continue to roll in every direction from the center of the fondant outward, to maintain an even thickness and achieve your desired measurement.

8 If you see any air bubbles in the fondant, insert a straight pin into them at an angle. Use your fingertips to gently guide the air out.

Caking Your First Steps

1

I **love new beginnings, don't you?** Starting your first caking project, just like starting anything new, can feel intimidating. I *still* get a little nervous when I'm caking something new. But then I remind myself that creativity takes courage and that if I break things down into small, simple steps, even the biggest challenge becomes manageable.

That's exactly why I've provided easy-to-follow, step-by-step instructions. I've divided the instructions for most of my cakes into two days or stages: the prep stage and then the decorating stage. Taking the time during the prep stage to measure out your ingredients and bake means that on decorating day, you're ready to go!

These are great starter cakes for any skill level, yet they're still showstoppers. Some are simpler spin-offs of my most popular cakes from YouTube, while other original cakes were inspired by requests from my YoYos.

For an added fun factor, try making these cakes with family and friends as a weekend project. They are a great way to practice your Yo Knows techniques, make an incredible cake, and create some sweet memories all at the same time. And isn't that the best thing about cake? We usually get to enjoy it when we're celebrating and spending time with the people we love. So call up your bestie or wrangle the fam to embark on an epic caking adventure. The cakes on these pages are your first steps.

Fried Chicken and Waffles

This is a great sweet treat to enjoy with family and friends as an extra-special Saturday morning breakfast or early-afternoon dessert. The perfect combination of textures and tastes comes together when you bite into the chicken and the waffle at the same time. You get that same delicious crunch from these sweet chicken pieces as you would from the real thing, while the soft, warm cake waffle is just YUM! And to top it all off, buttercream that looks like butter? I mean, really!

This is a perfect recipe for pranking your friends because nobody will be mad at you for tricking them. Just imagine the surprise on their faces when they dig into their diner-style Fried Chicken and Waffles—to discover they taste just like cake!

And even better? This is probably one of the least intimidating novelty cake recipes of all time. You don't even have to turn on your oven! So it's perfect for increasing your caking confidence, or getting kids comfortable in the kitchen. Just heat up your waffle iron, pour in your cake batter, and you're halfway to cake waffle heaven!

SERVES 2 TO 4

About 2 waffles and 2 pieces of chicken each

73

Fried Chicken and Waffles

⚒ Tools

Heatproof mixing bowls

Waffle iron

Silicone (heatproof) pastry brush

Mini ice cream scoop or melon baller

🥛 Ingredients

For the butter

¼ cup	Yo's Italian Meringue Buttercream (page 30)
	Gel food colorings: lemon yellow and golden yellow

For the chicken pieces

3 cups	puffed rice cereal
2 tablespoons	unsalted butter
8 ounces	mini marshmallows (half a 16-ounce bag)
½ teaspoon	pure vanilla extract
	Vegetable shortening
2 to 4	fat pretzel rods, broken into 2-inch lengths
2 cups	cornflake cereal
2 tablespoons	honey
2 tablespoons	glucose

For the waffles

½ recipe	Yo's Ultimate Vanilla Cake batter (page 24)
½ cup	whole milk (room temperature)
2 tablespoons	vegetable oil
	Pure maple syrup for serving

1. **Make the butter:** Prepare the buttercream according to the recipe. Put the buttercream in a bowl and use a toothpick to dab in the yellow food colorings a little at a time until you reach a buttery yellow color. Because butter has such a subtle yellow tint, you want to color gradually; it's useful to have real butter beside you as a color reference. Cover the bowl with plastic wrap and refrigerate.

2. **Make the chicken pieces:** Put the rice cereal in a heatproof bowl. Melt the butter in a small saucepan over medium heat. Add the marshmallows to the melted butter and stir with a wooden spoon, letting the marshmallows melt slowly. When the marshmallows are nearly melted with just a few lumps remaining, remove the pot from the heat and quickly stir in the vanilla.

3. Pour the hot marshmallow mixture over the rice cereal and stir until well combined.

If you can't get your chicken drumstick pieces just right, make chicken tenders instead!

4. Grease your hands with shortening to prevent sticking. Pull out a handful of the rice cereal mixture and compress and sculpt it into the shape of a chicken drumstick. At the top of the drumstick, insert a pretzel rod piece, then cover the rod with rice cereal mixture. To make wings, simply mold smaller handfuls of the mixture until you're happy with the shape. Put the pieces on a baking sheet lined with parchment paper and set aside at room temperature until they firm up, about 1 hour.

5. In a bowl, break up the cornflakes with your hands until they are coarse crumbs.

6. Stir together the honey and glucose. Brush the mixture over the chicken pieces, coating them completely. If the mixture is too thick, heat it in the microwave for a few seconds until it's thin enough to brush on—be warned, it's very sticky! Set aside to dry for about 10 minutes.

8 Make the waffles: Prepare the cake batter according to the recipe, then stir in the milk to thin it out.

7 Working with a few chicken pieces at a time, place them in the bowl of cornflake crumbs and gently press the crumbs around them to completely coat each piece. Set aside on the baking sheet.

9 Preheat a waffle iron. Brush the surface with oil and fill the waffle iron with batter according to the manufacturer's instructions. Cook until both the top and bottom of the waffle are golden brown. Transfer to a serving plate and repeat with the remaining batter.

10 Place chicken pieces on the waffles. Using a mini ice cream scoop or melon baller, scoop out the chilled buttercream to look like whipped butter. Place one or two balls on each serving. Drizzle with maple syrup, letting it pool in the squares of the waffles and around the chicken pieces. Serve this diner dish hot off the waffle iron any time of day!

Tacos

All right, so let's taco 'bout this cake for a second. My YoYos have been asking me to cake a taco for *years* now, but I just had to save it for this book. This simple cake is another great weekend baking project for kids—with a little bit of guidance, of course. They will love the fun of creating sweet tacos that look almost exactly like the real thing.

One thing I love about this recipe is that it transforms authentic soft tortillas into delightful dessert shells with a sweet cinnamon crunch. I thought about using fondant to create the shells, but using tortillas not only simplifies the caking process, it's also a wonderful alternative for people who don't love fondant.

The best part of this cake, though? Customizing your favorite toppings! I've suggested building the tacos with modeling chocolate "cheese" and "guacamole" buttercream, but you could set up a build-your-own taco cake bar. Whether it's Cinco de Mayo or Taco Tuesday, this cake will bring the fun to your fiesta any day of the year!

SERVES 4 TO 8

Tacos

1

CAKING YOUR FIRST STEPS

🔧 Tools

2 (6-inch) round cake pans (3 inches deep)

Sir Squeeze-A-Lot bottle (see page 52)

Serrated knife

Ruler

4 (10-inch) round cake boards

Small offset spatula

Pastry brush

Baking sheet

Sieve

Cheese grater

🧂 Ingredients

½ recipe	Yo's Ultimate Chocolate Cake batter (page 22)
¼ recipe	Yo's Dark Chocolate Ganache (page 36)
½ recipe	Yo's Simple Syrup (page 34)
¼ recipe	Yo's Modeling Chocolate (page 48)
	Gel food colorings: golden yellow, orange, buttercup yellow, and electric green
¼ cup	unsalted butter
½ cup	sugar
½ teaspoon	ground cinnamon
¼ teaspoon	ground allspice
¼ teaspoon	grated nutmeg
1 package (8-inch)	round flour tortillas
1 cup	dried coconut chips
½ cup	smooth red licorice bits
	Vegetable oil
4 ounces	light cocoa compound chocolate
4 ounces	dark cocoa compound chocolate
½ cup	small black or brown jelly beans
1 cup	cocoa puffed rice cereal
	Candy lime wedges

For the guacamole and sour cream (optional)

1½ cups	Yo's Italian Meringue Buttercream (page 30)
	Gel food colorings: avocado and leaf green

Day 1: Prep It

1 Preheat the oven to 350°F. Line the bottoms of two 6-inch round cake pans with parchment paper (see "How to Bake a Cake" on page 44).

2 Prepare the cake batter according to the recipe. Pour the batter into the prepared pans. Bake for 50 minutes, or until a toothpick inserted in the center comes out clean, rotating the pans halfway through. Transfer to wire racks and let cool completely in the pans. Cover tightly with plastic wrap and refrigerate overnight.

3 Prepare the ganache according to the recipe. Let cool completely at room temperature, then cover and set aside overnight.

4 Prepare the simple syrup according to the recipe. Let cool to room temperature. Pour into your Sir Squeeze-A-Lot bottle and refrigerate.

5 Prepare the modeling chocolate according to the recipe and color it to look like cheddar cheese, using golden yellow and orange food coloring. If you want to take it that extra step, pour the warm modeling chocolate into a rectangular mold, such as a silicone mini loaf pan, to cool and firm up into a cheese block shape. This is not necessary for the grating, but if you're assembling the "tacos" with friends, it's fun to make it look realistic.

6 If you're making the guacamole and sour cream, prepare the buttercream according to the recipe. Cover the bowl tightly with plastic wrap and refrigerate.

Day 2: Cake It

1 If you're making the guacamole and sour cream, remove the buttercream from the fridge and let it come to room temperature. This may take a few hours.

2 Remove the cakes from their pans and peel off the parchment. Set the cakes right side up, and level them using a serrated knife and ruler (see page 48). With the knife, cut each cake in half to make four semicircles.

3 Lay the cakes out on a clean work surface and shower them with simple syrup. Let the syrup soak in fully before continuing.

4 Put the cakes on four 10-inch round cake boards. Using a small spatula, crumb coat the sides and top of each semicircular cake with the ganache (see page 56). Transfer to the fridge to chill for 20 to 30 minutes, until the ganache is firm to the touch.

5 Flip the cakes over and crumb coat the other side. Return to the fridge for 20 to 30 minutes, until the ganache is firm to the touch. You won't ice these again, but you do need to make sure all sides are crumb coated and chilled.

6 **Make sweet taco shells:** Preheat the oven to 350°F. Melt the butter and whisk in ¼ teaspoon buttercup yellow food coloring. In a separate small bowl, mix together the sugar, cinnamon, allspice, and nutmeg.

7 Starting with two tortillas, brush the butter mixture on both sides of each tortilla, then sprinkle with the sugar spice mixture to coat the entire top surface of each tortilla. Place on a baking sheet lined with a nonstick baking mat or parchment paper and bake the two tortillas for 3 to 5 minutes, until golden. Have two of the semicircle cakes standing by and ready to go.

8 Remove the tortillas from the oven and let them cool on the baking sheet for just 1 to 2 minutes; they should be warm and flexible but not so hot that they'll melt the ganache off the cakes. Lay the tortillas sugar side down on a work surface and place one cake onto one half of each tortilla so the rounded edge of the cake is close to (but not lined up with) the edge of the tortilla. Lift the other side of the tortilla and fold it over the top of each cake. If a tortilla cracks as you fold it over a cake, and most of your crumb coat is removed, patch the crumb coat, and chill the cake. Prepare and bake a new tortilla, and try again.

9 Repeat with two more tortillas and the remaining two cakes.

Put a bit of vegetable oil on the blade of your knife to help keep candy from sticking to it as you cut.

10 Remove the modeling chocolate "cheese" from the fridge and turn it out of the mold if you used one. Place the modeling chocolate on a plate and place it in the freezer for about 30 minutes to firm up a little more before you grate it.

11 **Make lettuce:** In a bowl, dilute a tiny bit of electric green food coloring in ½ cup water. Add the coconut chips and give them a stir. Pour into a sieve to drain, then spread the tinted coconut chips on paper towels to dry.

12 **Make chopped tomatoes:** Dice the licorice bits into small pieces to look like diced tomato. If you're making the guacamole, set aside some of the tomato pieces.

13 **Make the ground beef and black bean mixture:** In a stainless steel bowl set over a pan of lightly simmering water, melt together the light and dark compound chocolate, stirring until smooth. Remove from heat. If you find that the mixture is starting to thicken too quickly, you can add about 1 teaspoon vegetable oil to soften it. Set a handful of the jelly beans aside and stir the remaining jelly beans and the rice puff cereal into the compound chocolate. Start to make your tacos right away, before the mixture sets.

14 Working quickly with one taco at a time, cover the exposed edge of each taco cake with the mixture; you can do this with a spoon. Before the mixture sets, sprinkle on some chopped "tomatoes" and press in a few of the reserved jelly beans. Sprinkle "lettuce" on top. Finally, grate some modeling chocolate "cheese" on the large holes of a cheese grater and sprinkle it on top. Repeat with the remaining tacos, reserving some of the "tomatoes" for the guacamole, if you're making it.

15 **Make the guacamole:** Color 1 cup of the buttercream with avocado and leaf green food coloring. Fold in the reserved "tomatoes" for texture and color, if desired. Leave the remaining ½ cup buttercream uncolored for "sour cream."

16 Serve the taco cakes with the guacamole, the sour cream, and candy lime wedges on the side for an extra-sweet fiesta.

To really spice up this cake, add a side of my cake nachos, which you can find on my YouTube channel.

Rainbow Grilled Cheese

1

CAKING YOUR FIRST STEPS

SERVES 4 TO 8

Makes 4 sandwiches

I have fun adding rainbows to cakes whenever I can—from mini-rainbow mega cakes to Thanksgiving Unicornucopias—but I think this rainbow-grilled goodness takes the cake!

This recipe—an easy-to-make twist on my classic Grilled Cheese cake—sandwiches pieces of rainbow-colored modeling chocolate "cheese" between slices of rich pound cake "bread" to create a simple yet show-stopping treat. The best part? Stacking your ingredients and frying them up like a real grilled cheese sandwich! Great for beginner bakers of all ages, this cake is fun, simple to make, and a sweet way to brighten up a rainy day with your family and friends.

The only tricky thing about this cake is figuring out a side to go with it. When I served my original grilled cheese cake with raspberry coulis ketchup on our YouTube channel, it unleashed a pretty heated debate between YoYos who dip their grilled cheese in ketchup and those who eat it with tomato soup. Personally, I like to enjoy mine with a tall, cool glass of pink lemonade!

Rainbow Grilled Cheese

1
CAKING YOUR FIRST STEPS

🔧 Tools

9 × 5 × 3½-inch loaf pan

7 small bowls

Nonstick mat or board

Small nonstick rolling pin

Ruler or fabric measuring tape

Pastry brush

Serrated knife

Frying pan

Pancake turner

🧃 Ingredients

For the pound cake

2⅓ cups	all-purpose flour
¾ teaspoon	table salt
1 cup (2 sticks)	unsalted butter, at room temperature
6 ounces	cream cheese, at room temperature
2 cups	sugar
¾ teaspoon	pure vanilla extract
4	large eggs, at room temperature

For the rainbow "cheese"

1½ recipes	Yo's Modeling Chocolate (page 44)
	Gel food colorings: red, orange, yellow, green, blue, purple, and pink (or your choice)

For assembly

½ recipe	Yo's Simple Syrup (page 34)
	Unsalted butter, softened

Day 1: Prep It

1 **Make the pound cake:** Preheat the oven to 350°F. Line the bottom and sides of a 9 × 5 × 3½-inch loaf pan with parchment paper (see "How to Bake a Cake" on page 44).

2 Sift together the flour and salt and set aside.

3 In a stand mixer fitted with the paddle attachment, begin to cream together the butter, cream cheese, sugar, and vanilla on low speed. Turn the speed to medium and beat until light and fluffy.

4 Return the mixer to low speed and continue to mix as you add the eggs, two at a time, mixing well after each addition. Gradually add the flour mixture, mixing until fully incorporated.

I added cream cheese to the cake because I like my grilled cheese extra cheesy!

5 Scrape the batter into the prepared loaf pan and spread so that it is smooth in the pan. Bake for about 2 hours, or until golden brown and a toothpick inserted in the center comes out clean, rotating the pan halfway through. Transfer to a wire rack and let cool completely in the pan. Cover tightly with plastic wrap and refrigerate overnight.

6 **Make the "rainbow cheese":** Make the modeling chocolate according to the recipe. Before it cools and solidifies, divide the melted chocolate mixture evenly among seven small bowls. Dye the mixture in each bowl a color of the rainbow—red, orange, yellow, green, blue, purple, and pink (or any shades you'd like). Let the chocolate cool to room temperature, then cover and let stand overnight.

Day 2: Cake It

1 Remove each color of modeling chocolate from its bowl and gently knead it before flattening it with your fingers as you would with fondant. On a nonstick mat or board, using a small nonstick rolling pin, roll each piece into a sheet ⅛ inch thick and a little more than 4 inches square. Stack the colors one on top of the other in the rainbow color order. Chill for about 30 minutes, or until the stack is firm.

2 Cut through your stack of colors to make thin slices. If the stack is soft when you start to slice it, put it back in the refrigerator until firm before continuing to slice. Arrange two slices side by side, with the rainbow showing, on a sheet of parchment paper. Top with a second sheet of parchment and roll them out until they form one slice that is slightly larger than 4 inches square. Repeat with the remaining slices, then chill the slices again until firm.

4 Remove the pound cake from the pan. Brush simple syrup on the top crust of the cake so it doesn't crack when sliced. (This is still cake, even though it looks like bread.) Using a serrated knife, trim off the ends, then cut eight ½-inch-thick slices from the cake.

You can re-roll your scraps to make marbled cheese slices.

3 Cut out perfect 4-inch squares to resemble cheese slices. Stack the rainbow cheese squares between small squares of parchment paper so that they look just like presliced cheese.

5 Generously butter one side of each cake slice. Assemble the rainbow grilled cheese cake just as you would a savory grilled cheese: lay one slice of pound cake buttered side down, top with two slices of rainbow modeling chocolate cheese, then finish with another slice of pound cake (buttered side up) on top.

6 Get a frying pan nice and hot over medium heat and fry the sandwiches until golden brown on each side, flipping with the pancake turner.

7 Cut each sandwich in half and watch the rainbow cheese ooze out. Serve hot and melty! Now you can say that you've caked the rainbow!

Pizza Slice

1

CAKING
YOUR FIRST
STEPS

Ah, pizza! Who doesn't love it!? Did you know pizza is actually ranked the number one food in the world? People say that it's basically happiness in food form, and I agree. It's always there for you and never disappoints you—and my Pizza Slice cake is no different! Since my husband, Mr. Cake, is Italian, I wanted to pay tribute to him and to his culture by including this simpler spin on my Pizza cake. Although he's usually the one who makes the pizza in our house, I'm the only one who can cake a pizza. And you can never have too much pizza, in any form, can you?

This cake will help you get comfortable with very simple cutting, carving, and fondant work, so it's perfect for beginners or supervised kids. The fun of this cake is using the brûlée torch to brown the crust, making it look like the real thing. I also love that every time you make it, you can change up the toppings. Whether you prefer your pizza Hawaiian-style using candied pineapple and "bacon" gummies, or a classic Margherita with modeling chocolate "cheese" and fondant "basil" pieces, you can always keep this pizza cake fresh—and you don't even have to wait for delivery!

SERVES 2 TO 4

Makes 2 large slices

Pizza Slice

1

CAKING YOUR FIRST STEPS

Tools

9 × 13-inch cake pan

Serrated knives (large and small)

Ruler or fabric measuring tape

Nonstick mat or board

Small nonstick rolling pin

Brûlée torch

Small offset spatula

2 (12-inch) cake boards

#12 round piping tip

Cheese grater

1½-inch circle cutter

Ingredients

For the cheese

½ recipe	Yo's Modeling Chocolate (page 48)

For the sauce

¼ cup	Yo's Italian Meringue Buttercream (page 30)
	Gel food colorings: red and crimson
2 tablespoons	seedless raspberry jam

For the crust

1 recipe	Yo's Ultimate Vanilla Cake batter (page 24)
12 ounces	white fondant
	Ivory gel food coloring

For the Hawaiian pizza toppings

	Vegetable oil
	Dried pineapple
	Strawberry Starburst candies (for ham)
	Strawberry mango fruit twists (for bacon)
	Black licorice cylinders (for olives)
1 (1-ounce) block	white chocolate (for Asiago cheese)
	Dried cranberries and yellow sugar confetti sprinkles (for chile flakes)

Day 1: Prep It

1 **Make the mozzarella cheese:** Prepare the modeling chocolate according to the recipe.

2 **Start the sauce:** Prepare the buttercream according to the recipe. Cover the bowl tightly with plastic wrap and refrigerate overnight.

3 **Start the dough:** Preheat the oven to 350°F. Line the bottom of a 9 × 13-inch cake pan with parchment paper (see "How to Bake a Cake" on page 44).

4 Prepare the cake batter according to the recipe. Scrape the batter into the prepared pan and spread so that it is smooth in the pan. Bake for 35 minutes, or until a toothpick inserted in the center comes out clean, rotating halfway through. Transfer to a wire rack and let cool completely in the pan. Cover tightly with plastic wrap and refrigerate overnight.

5 Color the fondant by kneading in ivory food coloring until you achieve a light crust color (see page 62). When the color is fully blended, form the fondant into a ball and wrap tightly in plastic wrap. Set aside in a cool, dry place.

Day 2: Cake It

1 Remove the buttercream from the fridge and let it come to room temperature. This may take a few hours.

2 Remove the cake from the pan and peel off the parchment. Set the cake right side up, and level it using a serrated knife and ruler so that it is 1 inch in height (see page 48). For this cake we'll leave the caramelization on the bottom, as it will look more like the bottom of a pizza slice.

3 **Cut two equal triangles from your cake:** Turn the cake so a long side is nearest you. With three long cuts, cut out two big triangles—your pizza slices—each with its short "crust" edge along the outer edge of the cake. You will have two smaller triangles on each side that you can enjoy as a snack!

4 Using a small serrated knife, round out the shortest side (where the caramelization is) to make a curved edge for the pizza crust.

6 While the cakes are chilling, finish the sauce: Stir red and crimson food coloring into the buttercream with a rubber spatula to achieve a bright red tomato sauce color. When you're happy with the color, whisk in the jam for texture. If the sauce looks clumpy, pop it in the microwave for 5 to 10 seconds and stir; this should help to smooth it out.

5 On a nonstick mat or board, using a small nonstick rolling pin, roll the fondant into two strips (one per slice) that are long enough to become the outer crust: each should be ¼ inch thick and about 2½ inches wide—wide enough to curl over the edge of your cake to look like a real pizza crust. Wrap the fondant around the curved crust edge, then use a paring knife to trim off any excess fondant from the ends. Make small indents with your fingers and thumbs to create a lifelike doughy crust texture. Put the cakes in the fridge to chill.

7 Now you're ready to brûlée your crust. Remove the cakes from the fridge and cover the exposed portions of the cake slices (the parts not covered with fondant) with clean cake pans. This will protect your cake from the heat. Use a brûlée torch to caramelize the fondant crust; don't hold it too close to the cake, and use a back-and-forth motion. Remove the cake pans and use a small paring knife to carve away any accidentally burned cake.

8 Use a small offset spatula to spread the tomato sauce buttercream on the cake slices, being careful not to get it on the caramelized crust. Feel free to put the slice on a cake board at this point to make it easier to work with.

9 Knead the modeling chocolate into a ball and place it in the freezer for about 30 minutes to firm up a little more before you grate it.

When cutting gummy candies, rub a bit of vegetable oil or vegetable shortening on your knife to keep it from sticking.

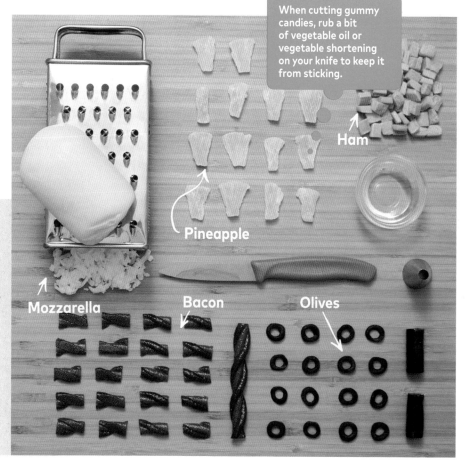

Ham

Pineapple

Mozzarella

Bacon

Olives

10 Prepare the toppings for my Hawaiian pizza (or see The Toppings Bar on page 100): With a paring knife, cut the pineapple pieces into smaller pieces and cut the Starburst candies into small cubes. Cut the fruit twists crosswise and horizontally. Cut black licorice into thin rounds, then use the piping tip to cut out an inner circle from each.

Cake research is important and delicious!

11 Grate the modeling chocolate on the large holes of a cheese grater and sprinkle it over the tomato sauce buttercream to make it look like mozzarella cheese. If the chocolate gets too warm to grate, put it back in the freezer for a bit before continuing to grate.

12 Sprinkle the pineapple, Starburst pieces, fruit twists, and licorice on the pizza cake slices, then top with a little more modeling chocolate cheese. Carefully brûlée the top to partially melt the chocolate cheese—just until it looks like cheese on a pizza.

13 As a finishing touch, finely grate the white chocolate over each slice for an "Asiago" effect and use chopped pieces of dried cranberries and confetti sprinkles as your chile flakes. Serve this while it's hot and fresh—just like the real thing!

The Toppings Bar

Make your favorite pizza!

Mix and match the toppings in this recipe with whatever lights your creativity (and taste buds) on fire!

- **Cheddar cheese:** Into modeling chocolate, blend sunset orange, lemon yellow, and golden yellow gel food coloring to achieve a cheesy color. Chill overnight.
- **Green olives:** Cut green licorice into thin rounds, then use the piping tip to cut out an inner circle from each.
- **Green peppers:** Thinly slice green wine gums.
- **Ground beef:** Melt together 2 tablespoons chopped dark chocolate and 2 tablespoons chopped milk chocolate. Stir in ½ cup cocoa puffed rice cereal.
- **Pepperoni:** Cut red fruit leather with a 1½-inch circle cutter.

Party Hat

SERVES 4 TO 6

Whether you're six or sixty-four, there's nothing quite like wearing a fun party hat on your birthday. That's why this Party Hat cake is the ultimate birthday cake for anyone, at any age! At *How To Cake It* we love a good celebration, and have been lucky to have so many things to celebrate! Now I'm throwing a party, and you're invited!

What's great about this cake is that the decorating possibilities are *endless*, and the true fun comes from creating your own unique designs and patterns. Try switching up the colors, adding stripes instead of stars, or covering the whole cake in sprinkles. But don't be sad when you have to cut into this cake—the colorful funfetti makes it a party on the inside, too!

This cake is a good one for bakers just starting out working with fondant because it teaches you how to cover a whole cake. If you're hosting a party or feeding a larger crowd, you can also use this cake as a decorative but edible cake topper—just set it on top of store-bought or simple round cake. Talk about caking your celebration to the next level!

Party Hat

1

CAKING YOUR FIRST STEPS

 Tools

10-inch square cake pan (3 inches deep)

Sir Squeeze-A-Lot bottle (see page 52)

Serrated knife

Ruler

Circle cutter set

10-inch round cake drum

Small offset spatula

Piping bag

#806 round piping tip

Rolling pins: wooden, French, and small nonstick

Fondant smoother

Nonstick mat or board

Star cutters or other shape (various sizes)

Paintbrushes

Herb scissors (or regular scissors)

Clay extruder with smallest round faceplate

Ingredients

1 recipe	Yo's Ultimate Vanilla Cake batter (page 24)
½ cup	rainbow sprinkles
½ recipe	Yo's Chocolate Swiss Meringue Buttercream (page 32)
½ recipe	Yo's Italian Meringue Buttercream (page 30)
½ recipe	Yo's Simple Syrup (page 34)
1 pound 12 ounces	white fondant
	Gel food colorings: yellow, red, orange, purple, blue, and green
	Confectioners' sugar for rolling fondant
	Yo's Royal Icing (page 38)
	Vegetable shortening
	Clear piping gel
	Pieces of raw spaghettini or spaghetti
	Silver luster dust

Day 1: Prep It

1 Preheat the oven to 350°F. Line the bottom of a 10-inch square cake pan with parchment paper (see "How to Bake a Cake" on page 44).

2 Prepare the cake batter according to the recipe. Gently fold in the sprinkles. (Add the sprinkles just before baking, so they don't bleed and muddle the color of the cake.) Scrape the batter into the prepared pan and spread so that it is smooth in the pan. Bake for 1 hour, or until a toothpick inserted in the center comes out clean, rotating the pan halfway through. Transfer to a wire rack and let cool completely in the pan. Cover tightly with plastic wrap and refrigerate overnight.

3 Prepare the two buttercreams according to the recipes. Cover each bowl tightly with plastic wrap and refrigerate.

4 Prepare the simple syrup according to the recipe. Let cool to room temperature. Pour into your Sir Squeeze-A-Lot bottle and refrigerate.

5 **Color fondant:** Divide 12 ounces of the fondant into six 2-ounce portions. Dye each a different color (see page 62): yellow, red, orange, purple, blue, and green. (Or you can use whatever colors you'd like.) Wrap each portion of fondant tightly in plastic wrap and set aside in a cool, dry place.

Day 2: Cake It

1 Remove the two buttercreams from the fridge and let them come to room temperature. This may take a few hours.

2 Remove the cake from the pan and peel off the parchment. Set the cake right side up, and level it using a serrated knife and ruler (see page 48). Flip the cake over and remove the caramelization from the bottom using the same technique.

3 Using six circle cutters (starting with the largest at 4½ inches and each subsequent cutter decreasing in diameter by ½ to ¾ inch), cut six circles from the cake. Later, when you stack the circles with the largest on the bottom and the smallest on top, it should form a natural cone shape.

4 Lay out all the cake pieces on a clean work surface and shower them with simple syrup, being careful not to oversaturate the smaller ones. Let the syrup soak in fully before continuing.

5 Place the largest circle on a 10-inch round cake drum. Turn the remaining five circles over so the simple syrup side is facing down, then use a small offset spatula to spread a layer of chocolate buttercream onto the tops of those five circles, maintaining a neat edge—you don't want any excess buttercream spilling off the sides. Stack the circles, turning each one upside down so that the buttercream side is placed on the layer underneath it. Once you have built up the cone, transfer it to the fridge to chill for 20 to 30 minutes, until the buttercream is firm to the touch.

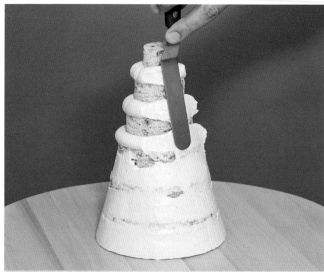

7 Use the small offset spatula to spread the piped buttercream, crumb coating the entire surface of the cake, following the natural slope of the cone. Pipe a dollop of buttercream on the top of the cone, where the point will be. Don't worry if the point isn't perfect now, as you'll be able to perfect it when you ice the cake. Transfer to the fridge to chill for 20 to 30 minutes, until the crumb coat is firm to the touch.

6 **Fill in the cone shape:** Fit a piping bag with a #806 round tip and fill it with Italian meringue buttercream. Pipe a ring of buttercream on the cake board around the edge of the bottom cake layer. Working your way from bottom to top, pipe a ring of buttercream onto the top edge of each cake round, hiding the chocolate buttercream.

8 Apply another layer of buttercream over the crumb coat, following the natural cone shape. Pay special attention to the top of the hat, shaping the buttercream to a nice point. Return it to the fridge to chill for 20 to 30 minutes, until the buttercream is firm to the touch. Smooth the icing with a little more buttercream if needed and chill again.

9 Measure the height of the cake and its circumference at the bottom. Dust a work surface with confectioners' sugar and, using a wooden rolling pin, roll out the white fondant until ⅛ inch thick and slightly larger than those measurements (see page 64).

10 To pick up the fondant, set the French rolling pin on one end of the fondant and roll the pin with the fondant around it (like wrapping paper onto a roll) until all the fondant is wrapped around the pin. Pick up the pin with the fondant wrapped around it, then quickly and carefully unroll it around the side of the cake, smoothing it out with a fondant smoother.

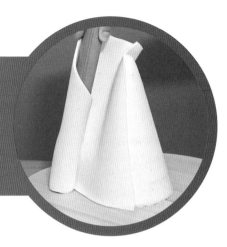

11 With a sharp paring knife, trim away the excess fondant, trimming at the top first before it peels back, and then trimming at the bottom. Where the ends of the fondant overlap, line up a ruler along the seam and use a sharp paring knife to cut through both layers of fondant; remove the excess from on top and underneath to create a clean seam. Try to get the tip of the cone neat, but don't worry too much about perfection here—it'll be partially obscured by the pom-pom, which will be easier to attach if the tip isn't too pointy. Knead together the fondant scraps, wrap them tightly, and set aside. Transfer the cake to the fridge while you work on the details.

12 **Create the star decorations:** On a nonstick mat or board, using a small nonstick rolling pin, roll out each of the colored fondants as thinly as possible. Using star cutters, cut out stars of different colors and sizes. I chose to cut the stars of each color the same size. (The party hat would also look great with polka dots or other shapes, so use any cutter shape you love.) Knead the scraps of each color into separate disks, wrap them tightly in plastic wrap, and set aside for the pom-pom.

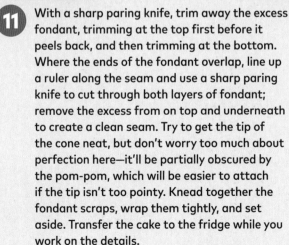

13 Attach the stars to the cake by lightly brushing water on the backs of the stars. I attached mine in a random pattern.

14 **Create the pom-pom:** Roll out each piece of colored fondant and cut into strips 1¼ inches wide and about 6 inches long. Fray one long edge of each strip using herb scissors, cutting a little more than halfway across the strip. (You can use regular scissors, but it will require more cuts and more patience.)

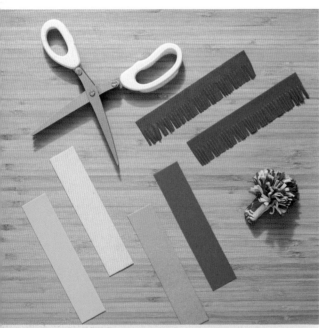

15 Glue the strips together by brushing water onto the unfrayed side and stacking them on top of one another with all the frayed edges on one side. Roll up the strips and squeeze them together just below the frayed parts. Pinch away the excess unfrayed fondant to make a pom-pom shape.

16 Carefully attach the pom-pom to the top of the cake with royal icing. For added security, you can push a piece of spaghettini through the pom-pom and into the cake to attach it.

17 **Make the string:** Knead a little vegetable shortening into a tiny bit of the remaining white fondant to soften it, then roll the fondant into a cord. Push the cord through a clay extruder using the smallest round faceplate to make a long string. Use some piping gel to attach the two ends of the strings to either side of the bottom of the party hat, about ½ inch up from the bottom. Let the remaining string drape across the cake drum.

18 **Create the staples:** Break off two ½-inch pieces of spaghettini. Brush with silver luster dust. (If it doesn't stick very well, lightly coat the spaghettini with shortening and brush again.) Apply to either side of the cake, just below the ends of the string, with a dot of piping gel. Now you're ready to party!

Giant Cake Slice

We all know that there are *many* different kinds of cake slices: the "just a taste" slice, the "it's my birthday" slice, the "broken-hearted so I'm going to need half the cake" slice, just to name a few. Well, I'd like to call this a Yo-sized cake slice (a.k.a. the whole cake)! And I can pretty much guarantee that if you bring this to a party, you'll have a slice.

Great for any type of occasion, this cake puts a sweet spin on my "Cake of Cakes" YouTube video, where I created a towering tiered cake of a cake stacked on top of a cake, stacked on top of a cake. And the top tier was, you guessed it, a slice of cake—with a cupcake on top. But this time, we're going BIG with a giant cake slice that's perfect for decorators looking to hone their fondant skills. With this cake you'll also get a crash course in measuring, which really comes in handy for the next level of cakes.

The fun of this cake is definitely in its jumbo size and bright party colors. And the oversized cherry on top is *literally* the cherry on top!

SERVES 10 TO 12

Giant Cake Slice

1

CAKING YOUR FIRST STEPS

Ingredients

1½ recipes	Yo's Ultimate Chocolate Cake batter (page 22)
1 recipe	Yo's Italian Meringue Buttercream (page 30)
1 recipe	Yo's Simple Syrup (page 34)
¾ pound	yellow fondant
½ pound	pink fondant
¼ pound	purple fondant
3 pounds	white fondant
	Gel food colorings: turquoise, red, and leaf green
2 ounces	gum paste
	Confectioner's sugar for rolling fondant
	Clear piping gel
	Vegetable shortening

Tools

11 × 15-inch cake pan

Sir Squeeze-A-Lot bottle (see page 52)

Pointed sculpting tool (cel stick)

Lollipop stick

18-gauge floral wire (for the cherry stem)

Nonstick mat or board

Small nonstick rolling pin

Paintbrush

Serrated knife

Ruler

16-inch square cake drum

Spatulas: small offset and medium straight

Fondant smoother

Clay extruder with half-moon faceplate

Day 1: Prep It

1 Preheat the oven to 350°F. Line the bottom of an 11 × 15-inch cake pan with parchment paper (see "How to Bake a Cake" on page 44).

2 Prepare the cake batter according to the recipe. Pour the batter into the prepared pan. Bake for 50 minutes, or until a toothpick inserted in the center comes out clean, rotating the pan halfway through. Transfer to a wire rack and let cool completely in the pan. Cover tightly with plastic wrap and refrigerate overnight.

3 Prepare the buttercream according to the recipe. Cover the bowl tightly with plastic wrap and refrigerate overnight.

4 Prepare the simple syrup according to the recipe. Let cool to room temperature. Pour into your Sir Squeeze-A-Lot bottle and refrigerate.

5 Now it's time to color the fondant. The yellow and pink fondants come precolored, so no prep there!

To lighten the purple fondant, mix the purple fondant with ¼ pound of the white fondant and knead to combine thoroughly.

To make teal fondant, mix ½ pound of the white fondant with turquoise food coloring and knead until evenly colored.

Wrap each ball of fondant individually in plastic wrap and set aside in a cool, dry place.

6 **Make the cherry:** Dye 1½ ounces of the gum paste red by adding red food coloring until it's the color of a cherry. Dye the rest of the gum paste using leaf green food coloring; set the green aside for now.

7 Roll the red gum paste into a ball (like an oversize cherry) and use the back of a knife to mark the indent line in the cherry, from the center of the top to the center of the bottom. Then use a pointed sculpting tool to make an indent where the stem will go. Using a lollipop stick, poke a hole halfway up through the bottom of the cherry. (Later you'll use the lollipop stick to affix the cherry to the cake.) Set aside to dry overnight.

8 **Make the cherry stem:** Cut a 3-inch length of floral wire to match the size of your cherry. On a nonstick mat or board, using a nonstick rolling pin, roll out a small piece of the green gum paste into a cord about an inch long and thicker than the wire. Brush a bit of piping gel onto the wire and push the wire up through the gum paste cord, twisting the wire while you insert it into the gum paste. Continue to roll and shape it a little in your hand to look like a stem. Trim away the bottom ½ inch or so of the gum paste to leave some wire exposed to fit into the cherry later on. Set aside to dry overnight.

9 **Make the sprinkles:** Roll ½ ounce of each of the colored fondants into thin cords. Cut the cords into even lengths with a paring knife, then use your index finger to roll each piece thinner. Let them curve slightly so the sprinkles look more realistic. Set aside to dry overnight.

Day 2: Cake It

❶ Remove the buttercream from the fridge and let it come to room temperature. This may take a few hours.

❷ Remove the cake from the pan and peel off the parchment. Set the cake right side up, and level it using a serrated knife and ruler (see page 48).

❸ Cut an M shape into the cake (as pictured in the photo) to make three large triangles and two half-triangles. Put together the two half-triangles to make a fourth triangle. Round out the shortest side of each triangle so it looks like it's been cut from a round cake. You may want to create a simple paper template to make sure all the pieces are the same shape.

❹ Lay out the four wedges on a clean work surface and shower them with simple syrup. Let the syrup soak in fully before continuing.

❺ Ice the top of three of the wedges with the buttercream. On a 16-inch square cake drum, set each wedge on its long side and sandwich all four wedges together, making sure they align. If the curved ends are uneven, trim them with the serrated knife.

6 Use a small offset spatula to crumb coat the cake with the buttercream (see page 56). Transfer to the fridge to chill for 20 to 30 minutes, until the crumb coat is firm to the touch.

7 Using a medium straight spatula, apply another layer of buttercream over the crumb coat, trying to get it as smooth as possible. Return it to the fridge for another 20 to 30 minutes, until the buttercream is firm to the touch.

8 Time for fondant! Measure one triangle side of the cake. On a nonstick mat or board, using a nonstick rolling pin and confectioners' sugar, roll out a piece of fondant the color you want for your bottom layer (I used yellow) that is large enough to cover that area. Cut one side of the rolled fondant into a straight line and press it against the cake with the straight edge flush against the cake drum. Trim away the excess with a sharp paring knife.

9 **Create fondant cake layers:** Measure the length and width of the top of your cake (the part that's meant to look like the side of the cake slice). Each band of fondant should be a bit longer than the top of your cake; divide the width of the cake by 4 to determine how wide each band should be. Roll out each of the four fondant colors and trim them to the width you determined.

10 Arrange the bands on the cake surface and smooth them with a fondant smoother. Trim any excess with a paring knife.

It's important to measure the bands carefully before you put them on the cake, because peeling them off and resizing them can get messy.

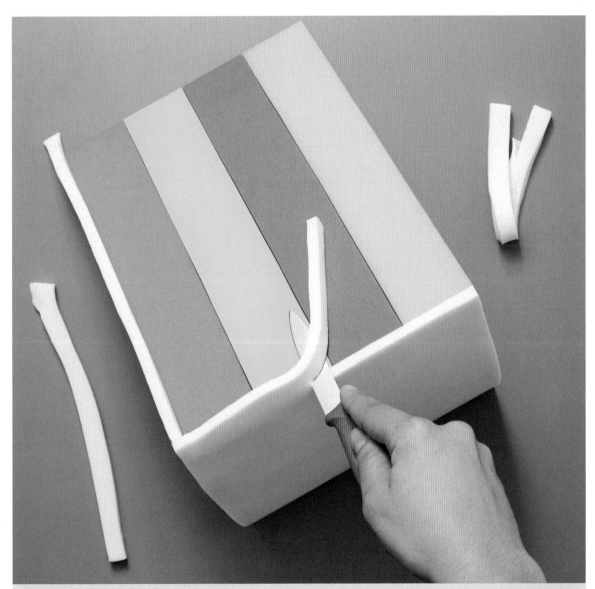

11 **Cover the rest of the cake:** Roll out white fondant until ¼ inch thick, measure and cut panels slightly larger than needed, apply them to the cake, and trim away any excess. When trimming the sides, make sure the slice is facing away from you as you're cutting so your hand doesn't brush against the colored fondant. Hold the blade of the knife flat on the cake and level with the angle of the cake slice.

13 Brush a little piping gel where the colored fondant bands meet on the side, then attach the cords, creating a slight wave in each one to give them a more realistic look.

14 **Make the swirl of "icing":** Roll some of the white fondant into a cord that's ½ inch thick and 20 inches long, then coil it up on itself. Apply to the cake using piping gel.

15 **Make fondant "piping":** Roll out another ½-inch-thick cord of white fondant, then cut it into 2½-inch pieces. Curl one end of each piece under to create a "wave" effect, then shape the trailing end of each wave on a slight angle to allow the next "wave" to sit snugly against it. Apply to the cake using piping gel.

16 Gently push the cherry stem into the gum paste cherry, then attach the whole cherry to the fondant icing swirl using the lollipop stick. Finally, attach sprinkles by dabbing a small amount of piping gel on each. Place sprinkles wherever you like—have fun with it!

12 **Make the "filling":** Mix the white fondant with a little shortening to soften it, then roll some of the fondant into four cords. Push each cord through a clay extruder using the half-moon faceplate. (You will only need three cords, but it's good to have an extra on hand in case one doesn't work out quite right.)

Watermelon

SERVES 12 TO 20

A **big reason I wanted** to start a YouTube channel was to be able to bake my "bucket list" of cakes— and this one was at the top of that list. What I didn't expect was that my Watermelon cake, better known as Walter Melon, would end up completely stealing the show. (His video is my most watched ever!) He became a recurring character on *How To Cake It* and even made the news around the world. Yup, he's pretty much a celebrity now, not to mention a diva. But that's not the only reason he made it into this book. He's actually the perfect project for practicing your cake painting skills, especially freehand patterns.

The real fun of this cake, though, is that it looks like a perfect, juicy watermelon both inside and out, with its white fondant rind, chocolate chip seeds, and pink velvet cake yumminess. I usually find it hard to cut into my cakes after I've put so much love and effort into them, but slicing this one is really satisfying. (Sorry, Walter!) You can even present it sliced for added fun. But don't be fooled: While Walter can act like a real melonhead sometimes, he's really quite sweet inside!

Watermelon

CAKING YOUR FIRST STEPS

 Tools

9-inch half-sphere cake pan (one half of a sphere pan set)

3 (9-inch) round cake pans (3 inches deep)

Kitchen scale

Sir Squeeze-A-Lot bottle (see page 52)

Serrated knife

Ruler and fabric measuring tape

14-inch round cake drum

Small offset spatula

Fabric measuring tape

Rolling pins: wooden and French

Fondant smoother

Paintbrushes

Ball and veining sculpting tools

Ingredients

1½ recipes	Yo's Pink Velvet Cake batter (page 26)
2 cups	semisweet chocolate chips
1 recipe	Yo's Italian Meringue Buttercream (page 30)
1½ recipes	Yo's Simple Syrup (page 34)
	Confectioners' sugar for rolling fondant
4 pounds	white fondant
	Gel food colorings: rose, red, moss green, kelly green, buttercup yellow, and ivory
	Clear food-grade alcohol

> You can bake in a 9-inch stainless-steel bowl instead of a half-sphere cake pan and line it the same way.

Day 1: Prep It

1 Preheat the oven to 350°F. Line a 9-inch half-sphere cake pan and the bottoms of three 9-inch round cake pans with parchment paper (see "How to Bake a Cake" on page 44). Set the half-sphere pan on a baking ring or a smaller cake pan set on top of a baking sheet to keep it upright.

2 Prepare the cake batter according to the recipe. You will add the batter to each pan in two parts, adding the chocolate chips in between. You will divide the batter and chocolate chips as follows:

3 (9-inch) round cake pans

¾ pound	batter each
¼ cup	chocolate chips each
¾ pound	batter each

9-inch   half-sphere pan

1½ pounds	batter
½ cup	chocolate chips
1½ pounds	batter

Pour the first half of the batter for each into the prepared pans as indicated above. Sprinkle the top of each pan of batter with chocolate chips, leaving a 1-inch border around the edge of the pan—because seeds are usually on the inside of the melon and not at the edge. Pour the second half of the batter into each of the pans as indicated above.

3 Bake the 9-inch round cakes for 40 minutes and the half-sphere cake for 1½ hours, or until a toothpick inserted in the center comes out clean, rotating the pans halfway through. Transfer to wire racks and let cool completely in the pans. Cover tightly with plastic wrap and refrigerate overnight.

4 Prepare the buttercream according to the recipe. Cover the bowl tightly with plastic wrap and refrigerate.

5 Prepare the simple syrup according to the recipe. Let cool to room temperature. Set aside a little syrup for the "watermelon juice" later, if you like. Pour the rest into your Sir Squeeze-A-Lot bottle and refrigerate.

> The chocolate chips will mostly sink to the bottom of the batter while baking, and that's okay—don't sweat it!

Day 2: Cake It

1 Remove the buttercream from the fridge and let it come to room temperature. This may take a few hours.

2 Remove the 9-inch round cakes from the pans and peel off the parchment. Set the cakes right side up, and level them using a serrated knife and ruler (see page 48). It can be difficult to cut through chocolate chips, so take your time. Flip the cakes over and remove the caramelization from the bottoms using the same technique. Remove the sphere cake from the pan and level the flat side, being sure to remove the caramelization.

3 Lay out all the cakes on a clean work surface and shower them with simple syrup, showering both the flat and curved sides of the sphere cake. Let the syrup soak in fully before continuing.

4 Divide the buttercream evenly between two bowls. Color one half of the buttercream the same color as the cakes, using rose and red food coloring. Set the remaining white buttercream aside.

5 Place one 9-inch cake on a 14-inch round cake drum. Using a small offset spatula, spread a thin layer of watermelon-colored buttercream onto the cake. Sprinkle ¼ cup of the remaining chocolate chips over the buttercream, again leaving a 1-inch border at the edge. Add another dollop of buttercream and spread over the chocolate chips. Stack and fill the other two round cakes on top, using the remaining chocolate chips and more buttercream. Place the sphere cake, dome side up, on top of the stacked cakes. Transfer to the fridge to chill for 20 to 30 minutes, until the buttercream is firm to the touch.

6 With the serrated knife, carve away all the caramelization from the cakes, starting at the top and working downward, maintaining the dome shape. Avoid overcarving—this cake already has a natural watermelon shape, so just remove anything that's too dark.

7 Use the offset and straight spatulas to crumb coat the cake with the white buttercream (see page 56). Transfer to the fridge to chill for 20 to 30 minutes, until the crumb coat is firm to the touch.

8 Apply another layer of white buttercream over the crumb coat, trying to get it as smooth as possible. Return it to the fridge to chill for 20 to 30 minutes, until the buttercream is firm to the touch.

9 **Make the watermelon rind:** Measure the cake, from the bottom of one side, up and over to the bottom of the other. Dust the work surface with confectioners' sugar and, using a wooden rolling pin, roll out a circle of fondant that is ½ inch thick and large enough to cover the cake. Set a French rolling pin in the center of the fondant and fold one end up over it. Try not to handle the fondant too much. Pick up the pin, then quickly and carefully drape the fondant over the cake. Use a fondant smoother and your hands to smooth it over the cake. Trim away excess fondant at the base of the cake with a sharp paring knife.

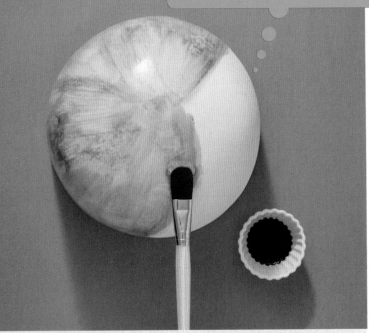

Start by making a small batch of paint to test on a spare piece of fondant. If your green is too dark, remove some of the paint from your bowl and add more alcohol. If it's too light, add a little more green.

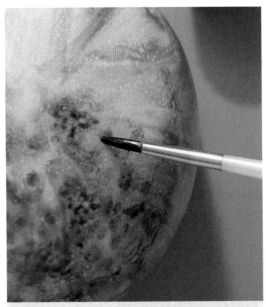

10 To make realistic-looking watermelon skin, you'll need to paint the fondant in several layers, letting each dry before starting the next. Begin with a light green shade as the base coat: In a small bowl, mix moss green, kelly green, buttercup yellow (to make the green more subtle and natural), and just a touch of red food coloring (to dull the color) and dilute it with a bit of clear food-grade alcohol. Using a paintbrush, paint a base coat to cover the entire cake, using downward brushstrokes. Let dry completely, about 30 minutes.

11 For these next steps, it's helpful to have a real watermelon nearby to get the right shades and patterns. Add more moss green to the paint mixture you just used, deepening the color. Dot the cake all over to create a speckled pattern. Let dry completely, about 30 minutes.

13 With the darkest paint, add darker areas of speckling like a real watermelon would have. Let dry completely, about 30 minutes.

Real watermelons have imperfections—that is, areas where there are more speckles and where the lines aren't so pronounced.

12 Darken the color further with more moss green, and paint darker stripe-like patterns on the cake, one at a time, working down from the top center. Then use a drier brush to dab and soften the stripe pattern.

15 I like to serve this cake with a slice removed to reveal the chocolate chip seeds. I also like to gently push additional chocolate chip seeds into the cake to give it a more realistic look.

16 It's also fun when you're plating this cake to leave a little drizzle of "watermelon juice" around the bottom. You can create this by mixing just a touch of rose food coloring into some of the reserved simple syrup. Now you, too, can enjoy your very own juicy watermelon!

14 **Add the flower stalk:** Use a ball tool to gently push an indent into the top center of the cake. Roll a small piece of white fondant into a ball and pop it into the indentation. Add some texture by pressing around the fondant with a pointed veining tool. Paint the stalk with a bit of ivory food coloring diluted with alcohol. Let dry completely.

Cake It Up
a Notch

2

Yay! You caked it! You've caked your first steps and have completed the previous seven sensational creations.
If I was in your kitchen with you now I'd give you a big spatula high-five. What's that? It's something my son invented—we each hold a spatula and high-five in celebration. So spatula high-fives for caking your skills to the next level.

By now you're comfortable with simple syruping, crumb coat and chilling, and working with fondant. In the pages ahead we're going to cake things up a notch with larger cakes of different shapes that require more sculpting and carving. I picked these cakes because their shapes are forgiving and not too intricate, so they're perfect for practicing basic carving and for increasing your fondant confidence. You'll also master fondant and gum paste detailing.

Don't worry—this isn't just about building skills. These seven cakes are extra fun and extra special—and they will really wow your guests (and you!).

Try these cakes in the order they are laid out, as each is a little more challenging than the last. But if you feel inspired to dive in and try a specific cake—go for it! Now that you have the basics down, it's time to be bold with your caking goals. Remember, failure isn't the opposite of success; it's a part of it. If you make a mistake, you'll just end up with a lot of cake scraps, which isn't so bad, right? So let's get ready to cake it up!

Jumbo Candy Apple

SERVES 6 TO 8

Whenever I walk by a display of candy apples, I *always* stop to look—there's just something about the colors and textures that catches my attention. So I thought it would be fun to show you how to cake a jumbo one. What I love most about this cake is that there's so much room to get creative with it. You can dress it up for a theme or a season by adding a different colored ribbon or bows to the stick, just like real candy apples. Or, if you're giving it as a gift, you can decorate it with the recipient's favorite colors and candies.

Most of my novelty cakes are covered in fondant, but I love how with this cake, in addition to fondant that makes it look like a real apple, we use chocolate and candy to enhance the outside to make it look like the real thing—and to add a ton of yummy flavor. And the other thing that makes it the apple of my eye? It's still a pretty easy design to cake—so it will help you improve your carving skills. In fact, the hardest part about making this cake is trying not to eat all the toppings before you're done.

Jumbo Candy Apple

 Ingredients

1 recipe	Yo's Ultimate Vanilla Cake batter (page 24)
½ recipe	Yo's Italian Meringue Buttercream (page 30)
½ recipe	Yo's Simple Syrup (page 34)
1 pound	white fondant
	Gel food colorings: avocado, electric green, crimson, white, and yellow
	Confectioners' sugar for rolling fondant
	Clear food-grade alcohol

For the toppings

7	candy bars
2 ounces	dark cocoa compound chocolate
½ cup	candy-coated chocolates (such as M&M's)

For the "caramel"

4 ounces	light milk compound chocolate
4 ounces	orange compound chocolate
2 teaspoons	vegetable oil
	Gel food colorings: yellow and orange

Tools

6-inch sphere cake pan (both halves)

Sir Squeeze-A-Lot bottle (see page 52)

Serrated knives (large and small)

10-inch round cake drum

Small offset spatula

Rolling pins: wooden and French

Straight pin

Small paintbrush

Parchment piping bags

½-inch-wide × 12-inch-long wooden cake dowel, sharpened at one end

Ribbon

Day 1: Prep It

1 Preheat the oven to 350°F. Line the pans with parchment paper (see "How to Bake a Cake" on page 44). Set the pans on baking rings or smaller cake pans set on top of a baking sheet to keep them upright.

2 Prepare the cake batter according to the recipe. Scrape the batter into the prepared pans and spread so that it is smooth in the pans. Bake for 1 hour, or until a toothpick inserted in the center comes out clean, rotating the pans halfway through. Transfer to a wire rack and let cool completely in the pans. Cover tightly with plastic wrap and refrigerate overnight.

> Put the sphere pans on a baking sheet to catch any possible spillover as the cake batter rises in the oven. Candy apple cakes are fun, but cleaning the oven is not!

3 Prepare the buttercream according to the recipe. Cover the bowl tightly with plastic wrap and refrigerate.

4 Prepare the simple syrup according to the recipe. Let cool to room temperature. Pour into your Sir Squeeze-A-Lot bottle and refrigerate.

5 **Dye the fondant a green apple hue:** Knead avocado, electric green, and a tiny dot of crimson food coloring into the white fondant (see page 62) to make a green apple color—you want to use just enough crimson to dull the green slightly but not turn the fondant brown. Wrap the fondant tightly in plastic wrap and set aside in a cool, dry place.

> Food coloring is very bright, so natural colors like that of a green apple can be hard to recreate. Here's my trick to tone down the brightness: add a touch of coloring that contrasts the main color you're working with. For example, adding a bit of red tones down green.

Day 2: Cake It

1 Remove the buttercream from the fridge and let it come to room temperature. This may take a few hours.

2 With the cakes still in their pans, use a serrated knife to level them, using the cake pan rim as a guide.

3 Remove the cakes from their pans and peel off the parchment. Cut a thin slice off the domed side of one cake (which will become the bottom of the apple) so that the cake doesn't wobble. Set it on a 10-inch round cake drum. Top with the other cake to form a sphere, then carve the sphere into an apple shape using a small serrated knife. Be sure to carve away all the caramelization. Use a real apple as a model. Take your time when carving. You can always take a little more off, but you can't stick it back on.

4 Once you're happy with the shape, pull the halves apart and shower them on all sides with simple syrup. Let the syrup soak in fully before continuing.

5 Sandwich together the top and bottom of your apple with a layer of buttercream.

6 Carve out a little indentation where the stem would be with a small serrated knife.

7 Use a small offset spatula to crumb coat the cake with some of the buttercream (see page 56). Transfer the cake to the fridge to chill for 20 to 30 minutes, until the crumb coat is firm to the touch.

8 Apply another layer of buttercream over the crumb coat, trying to get it as smooth as possible. Return it to the fridge for 20 to 30 minutes, until the buttercream is firm to the touch.

9 Smooth out any ridges in the buttercream with small a spatula or slightly wet fingertips.

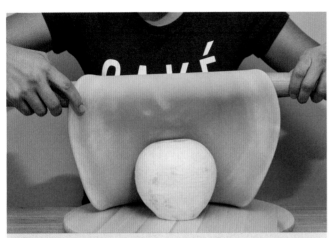

10 Dust the work surface with confectioners' sugar and, using a wooden rolling pin, roll out the green fondant until ⅟₁₆ inch thick and large enough to cover your cake. Set a French rolling pin in the center of the fondant and fold one end up over it. Try not to handle the fondant too much. Pick up the pin, then quickly and carefully drape the fondant over the cake.

11 Once the fondant is on the cake, smooth it over the curves of the apple with your hands. You'll notice that some air will get trapped in the top; prick the fondant with a straight pin and gently press out the air. Continue to smooth all the way around, tucking the fondant under the cake and trimming away any excess with a sharp paring knife.

You can test your paint color on any leftover green fondant.

12 In a small bowl, combine a drop each of avocado, white, and yellow food coloring and dilute them with alcohol. If the mixture gets lumpy, strain it through a paper towel or cheesecloth. With a small paintbrush and using downward brush strokes, paint from the top of the apple about halfway down to mimic the look of apple skin—this is a great project for practicing your fondant painting skills.

13 **Prepare the toppings:** Cut the candy bars in half lengthwise and then thinly slice each half crosswise. Make sure your slices are thin, so they won't fall off the apple.

14 **Make the "caramel":** In a stainless steel bowl set over a pan of lightly simmering water, melt together the milk and orange compound chocolate, stirring until smooth. Stir in the vegetable oil and yellow and orange food coloring to make a caramel color, then pour into a parchment piping bag.

16 Now it's time to place the candy-bar pieces on the apple. Working quickly before the mixture hardens, pipe a dot of the "caramel" on each slice of candy bar and stick it to the cake.

17 In a stainless steel bowl set over a pan of lightly simmering water, melt the dark compound chocolate, stirring until smooth, then pour into a parchment piping bag. Cut open the tip, drizzle the mixture over the cake, and stick on the candy-coated chocolates.

18 Press the sharp end of the dowel into the indentation in the top of the cake. Tie a pretty ribbon on the end as a final touch!

15 Cut open the tip of the piping bag and pipe a line of the "caramel" around the cake about two-thirds of the way up the side (don't hide too much of your pretty green!). As you pipe, use a small offset spatula to spread the mixture smoothly down to the bottom of the apple, so it looks like it is covered in caramel.

Sand Pail

2

CAKE IT UP A NOTCH

SERVES 12 TO 16

Summer is hands down my favorite season: the season of watermelon, ice cream, and my birthday (Mr. Cake's birthday, too!). I live in Toronto, Canada, where the winters can be very long and cold, so when the warm weather rolls in and the sun starts shining, my heart sings like Bey in concert. So for all my fellow summer lovers, this cake is for you.

This cake is especially fun to serve in the middle of winter, when everyone is missing the sun and craving sweet treats. It also makes a great birthday cake for kids, as most of them love the beach and playing in the sand. We took our son to the beach on our first family vacation, and he was completely fascinated with the sand, scooping it for hours and hours. With this cake you get to play with sand, too, only this sand is made with brown sugar and graham cracker crumbs. It's also fun to create seashells out of gum paste. You can customize your sand pail, using your favorite colors or creating patterns or designs on the pail that someone special would love. However you slice it, this cake will have you feeling like you're on vacaketion!

Sand Pail

2

CAKE IT UP A NOTCH

Tools

4 (6-inch) round cake pans

Sir Squeeze-A-Lot bottle (see page 52)

Nonstick mat or board

Rolling pins: small nonstick, wooden, and French

Circle cutters: 1-inch and 4½-inch

#807 round piping tip

Silicone seashell molds

¼-inch-wide × 12-inch-long wooden cake dowel

Paintbrushes

Serrated knife

Ruler

2 (10-inch) round cake boards

Small offset spatula

Fondant smoother

Masking tape

Ingredients

1½ recipes	Yo's Ultimate Vanilla Cake batter (page 24)
½ recipe	Yo's Italian Meringue Buttercream (page 30)
	Turquoise gel food coloring
1 recipe	Yo's Simple Syrup (page 34)
1 pound	gum paste
	Vegetable shortening
	Clear piping gel
	Confectioners' sugar for rolling fondant
1½ pounds	purple fondant
2 cups	packed light brown sugar
1 cup	graham cracker crumbs
	Luster dust: pink and pearl
¼ recipe	Yo's Royal Icing (page 30)

Day 1: Prep It

1 Preheat the oven to 350°F. Line the bottoms of three 6-inch round cake pans with parchment paper (see "How to Bake a Cake" on page 44).

2 Prepare the cake batter according to the recipe. Scrape the batter into the prepared pans and spread so that it is smooth in the pans. Bake for 1 hour, or until a toothpick inserted in the center comes out clean, rotating the pans halfway through. Transfer to wire racks and let cool completely in the pans. Cover tightly with plastic wrap and refrigerate overnight.

3 Prepare the buttercream according to the recipe. Put 2 cups of the buttercream in a bowl and stir in turquoise food coloring to make a bright teal color. Cover both bowls of buttercream (colored and uncolored) tightly with plastic wrap and refrigerate.

4 Prepare the simple syrup according to the recipe. Let cool to room temperature. Pour into your Sir Squeeze-A-Lot bottle and refrigerate.

5 **Make the pail handle:** On a nonstick mat or board, using a nonstick rolling pin, roll out 2 ounces of the gum paste into a band about 18 inches long, then cut it into a ½-inch-wide strip. With the band on its side, bend it around the curve of a 6-inch cake pan. Let dry around the pan overnight.

It's always a good idea to make extra gum paste pieces, because they can break easily.

6 Roll out a little more gum paste. Cut two circles using the 1-inch circle cutter, and then cut out the middle of each circle with the piping tip to make rings.

7 **Make the seashells:** Rub a little bit of shortening into a silicone seashell mold. Press a small amount of gum paste into each mold, then remove them. I made about 20 shells. Set aside to dry.

8 **Make the shovel:** Cut the dowel into two pieces, a 2-inch piece that will serve as the shovel handle and a 10-inch piece for the shaft of the shovel.

9 Dye 2 ounces of gum paste bright teal by adding turquoise food coloring. Roll out one piece long enough to fully cover the short dowel. Brush the dowel with clear piping gel, then wrap the teal gum paste around it. Trim any excess gum paste where it meets. Roll the dowel on a clean work surface to ensure the gum paste is smooth. Smooth the excess gum paste over the ends to cover it fully and trim away any excess.

10 Roll out another piece of gum paste large enough to cover one-third of the long dowel. Brush the dowel with clear piping gel, then wrap the teal gum paste around it. Trim any excess gum paste where it meets. Roll the dowel on a clean work surface to ensure the gum paste is smooth. Trim away any excess gum paste from the top end.

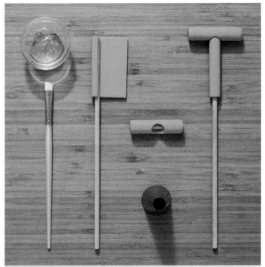

11 On the center of the seam on the smaller dowel piece, use the piping tip to cut a circle from the gum paste. This will create a spot for the two shovel pieces to fit together once they're dry. Set the shovel pieces aside to dry overnight.

Day 2: Cake It

1 Remove both buttercreams from the fridge and let them come to room temperature. This may take a few hours.

2 Remove the cakes from the pans and peel off the parchment. Set the cakes right side up, and level them using a serrated knife and ruler (see page 48). Flip the cakes over and remove the caramelization from the bottoms using the same technique.

3 Using the serrated knife and ruler, cut the cakes in half horizontally to make two cake layers. Lay out all the cakes on a clean work surface and give them all a light shower of simple syrup. Let the syrup soak in fully before continuing.

4 On a 10-inch round cake board, stack and fill the cakes, spreading a dollop of turquoise buttercream over the bottom five layers with a small offset spatula. (Do not spread buttercream on the top cake layer.) When your cake is six layers high, all filled with buttercream, transfer it to the fridge to chill for 20 to 30 minutes, until the buttercream is firm to the touch.

5 On the top center of the stack of cake (which will be the bottom of your pail once the cake is flipped upright), mark a 4½-inch circle with a circle cutter or place a template cut to the same diameter on top. With a serrated knife, carve in an A-line cut to the outside edge of the base of the cake, carving all around.

6 When you're happy with your pail shape, use a small offset spatula to crumb coat the side of the cake with some of the uncolored buttercream (see page 56). Transfer the cake to the fridge to chill for 20 to 30 minutes, until the crumb coat is firm to the touch.

7 Apply another layer of buttercream over the crumb coat, trying to get it as smooth as possible. Return it to the fridge for 20 to 30 minutes, until the buttercream is firm to the touch.

8 Measure the height of the cake and its circumference at the bottom. Dust the work surface with confectioners' sugar and, using a wooden rolling pin, roll out a sheet of purple fondant until ⅛ inch thick and large enough to wrap around (not drape over) the cake to cover the sides.

9 To pick up the fondant, set the French rolling pin on one end of the fondant and roll the pin with the fondant around it (like wrapping paper onto a roll) until all the fondant is wrapped around the pin. Pick up the pin with the fondant wrapped around it, then quickly and carefully unroll it around the side of the cake, smoothing it out with a fondant smoother. Where the ends of the fondant overlap, line up a ruler along the seam and use a sharp paring knife to cut through the overlapping fondant. Remove the excess from on top and underneath to create a clean seam. Trim away any excess at the top and the bottom.

10 Roll out another piece of purple fondant long enough to go around the circumference of the bottom of your cake (which will be the rim of the pail). Cut a ¼-inch-wide strip and attach it to the bottom of the cake with a little bit of water and a paintbrush.

11 Using the piping tip, cut out two circles from the purple fondant trimmings. Set these aside.

12 Center a 10-inch cake board upside down on top of the cake. Put one hand underneath the bottom cake board and one hand on top of the top cake board; holding the cake firmly but without squeezing it, quickly flip the cake right side up. Remove the cake board from the top.

13 Add some details to your bucket by marking a few indents around the base of the bucket. (I created three lines by lightly dragging rulers around the cake to mark indents in the fondant.)

14 Mix together the brown sugar and graham cracker crumbs to make a sweet sand, and sprinkle some of it on top of the pail, being sure to cover any exposed cake. Spread the remaining sand around the base of the pail to make it look like it's sitting on the beach.

This cake is buckets of fun!

15 Dry-brush your dried gum paste seashells with a bit of pink and pearl luster dust. (Tip: I do this on a paper towel, one color at a time, as it helps to save and reuse the luster dust.) Arrange them in the sand around the base of the cake and in the sand on top of the cake.

16 Use a bit of royal icing to affix each end of the white gum paste handle to the cake. Use the royal icing to stick a white gum paste ring over each end of the handle, and then stick the purple circles in the middle to make it look like the handle is attached to the pail.

17 Gently press the shaft of the shovel into the top of the cake deep enough to bury the exposed wooden dowel. If this causes the sand to shift, build it back up around the pail handle. Using royal icing, stick the short dowel piece (the shovel handle) onto the large dowel piece, lining up the shaft with the hole cut in the handle's gum paste.

Piggy Bank

SERVES 12 TO 15

Who didn't cherish their piggy bank growing up? I actually still have my childhood piggy bank—it's where I save coins I collect from around the world. (See, I told you I was sentimental!) But what really inspired this cake is my son's love of his own piggy bank. He'd be thrilled if I caked him a piggy bank cake, and I'm sure there are lots of other little kids out there who would feel the same way.

This cake is an especially good option for a baby shower or toddler's birthday because of what I call the "sculpting-to-cuteness ratio": it requires minimal sculpting but delivers maximum cuteness. It's also a perfect cake for practicing fondant details and modeling those adorable piggy parts. Get creative with your piggy's color or facial expressions. I made my piggy look up at the coin going in above, but you could have him wink. The real payoff of this cake? Breaking it open to enjoy what's inside!

Piggy Bank

2

CAKE IT
UP A
NOTCH

Ingredients

2 recipes	Yo's Ultimate Chocolate Cake batter (page 22)
½ recipe	Yo's Italian Meringue Buttercream (page 30)
	Soft pink gel food coloring
1 recipe	Yo's Simple Syrup (page 34)
1 ounce	black fondant
	Confectioners' sugar for rolling fondant
3 pounds	pink fondant
	CMC powder
	Clear piping gel
1 ounce	gum paste
	Pieces of raw spaghetti
	Luster dust: pink, pearl, silver, and gold
	Clear food-grade alcohol
	Chocolate coins

Tools

9-inch sphere cake pan (both halves)

Sir Squeeze-A-Lot bottle (see page 52)

Serrated knife

14-inch round cake drum

Spatulas: small offset and small straight

Nonstick mat or board

Rolling pins: small nonstick, wooden, and French

2-inch oval cutter

Fabric measuring tape

Fondant smoother

Straight pin

Ball sculpting tool

Letter "I" cutter

Paintbrushes

#807 round piping tip

Cell stick or pointed sculpting tool

Day 1: Prep It

1 Preheat the oven to 350°F. Line both half-sphere pans with parchment paper (see "How to Bake a Cake" on page 44). Set the pans on baking rings or smaller cake pans set on top of a baking sheet to keep them upright.

2 Prepare the cake batter according to the recipe. Pour the batter into the prepared pans. Bake for 2 hours, or until a toothpick inserted in the center comes out clean, rotating the pans halfway through. Transfer to a wire rack and let cool completely in the pans. Cover tightly with plastic wrap and refrigerate overnight.

3 Prepare the buttercream according to the recipe. Stir in food coloring to color it soft pink. Cover the bowl tightly with plastic wrap and refrigerate.

4 Prepare the simple syrup according to the recipe. Let cool to room temperature. Pour into your Sir Squeeze-A-Lot bottle and refrigerate.

Day 2: Cake It

1 Remove the buttercream from the fridge and let it come to room temperature. This may take a few hours.

2 Remove the cakes from their pans, and set them curved side down (like a bowl). Use a serrated knife to level the tops. Make sure both half-spheres are leveled to the same height.

3 Create an oval template out of paper that mimics the shape of a piggy bank. The oval should be about 7¾ inches long and 6¾ inches wide. Place one of the half-spheres round side down, then center the template on the flat side. Using a paring knife, cut about 1 inch straight down into the cake, following the template. Remove the template and flip the cake over (flat side down). Holding your knife parallel to your working surface, cut into the cake 1 inch up from the flat base, so that you are meeting the previous cut at a right angle, cutting all the way around. Remove the excess cake you just cut, revealing the oval cross-section of your piggy bank. Use the serrated knife to carve the dome into an oval dome shape, making sure your cuts meet up with the oval shape at the base. Repeat with the second half-sphere.

4 When you're happy with the shape of each half, stack them with the flat sides together and, if needed, trim with the serrated knife to ensure that the two halves make a smooth oval shape.

5 Separate the halves, place them on a clean work surface, and shower both the flat and curved sides of each with simple syrup. Let the syrup soak in fully before continuing.

6 Place one half-sphere, flat side up, on a 14-inch round cake drum. With a small offset spatula, spread some of the buttercream over the flat side, spreading it to the edges. Place the second half-sphere on top, flat side down. If the cake feels wobbly (its own weight should be enough to keep it from rolling), you can trim a very thin sliver off the bottom to stabilize it.

7 Use the offset spatula to crumb coat the cake with some of the buttercream (see page 56). Transfer to the fridge to chill for 20 to 30 minutes, until the crumb coat is firm to the touch.

8 Apply another layer of buttercream over the crumb coat, trying to get it as smooth as possible. Return it to the fridge to chill for 20 to 30 minutes, until the buttercream is firm to the touch.

9 If there are any ridges in the buttercream, smooth them out with your wet fingertips or add a touch more buttercream with the spatula.

10 On a nonstick mat or board, using a small nonstick rolling pin, roll out the black fondant as thinly as possible. With a sharp paring knife, cut out a rectangle that is 1 × 3 inches to go on the pig's back where the coin slot would be. Set it at the top center of the pig's back and smooth it onto the buttercream to secure it.

When you cover your piggy bank in pink fondant and then cut a slit out of the pink, you'll see black as if it were hollow.

11 **Make the pig's nose:** Roll out 1 ounce of the pink fondant until ½ inch thick and use a 2-inch oval cutter to cut out an oval. Center the oval on one end of the cake and secure it by pressing it into the buttercream.

12 Measure the whole cake, from the base of one end, over the top, to the base of the other end, then from the base of one side, over the top, to the base of the other side. Dust the work surface with confectioners' sugar and, using a wooden rolling pin, roll out a slab of the pink fondant to a circle that is ¼ inch thick and wide enough that it can cover the entire cake.

13 Set a French rolling pin in the center of the fondant and fold one end up over it. Try not to handle the fondant too much. Pick up the pin, then quickly and carefully drape the fondant over the cake, smoothing it over the sphere and around the nose with your hands and a fondant smoother. Tuck and press the fondant into the curve near the bottom. If air gets trapped around the nose area, gently release it by piercing with a straight pin and continue smoothing. With a domed cake, it's natural to get folds at the bottom; don't worry—just keep smoothing.

14 Trim away excess fondant at the piggy's underbelly with a sharp paring knife. Don't worry about any creases—you will have a chance to repair them later. Transfer the cake to the fridge to chill for 20 minutes.

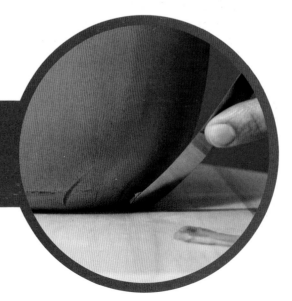

15 Repair any creases at the bottom: Make a fondant paste by mixing some pink fondant with water until it's spreadable. Using a small straight spatula, smooth a small amount of paste over the creases.

16 To create the piggy's nostrils, use a ball sculpting tool to make two impressions on the nose.

17 Cut out the coin slot at the top center of your cake where you put the black fondant rectangle, being careful to cut through only the pink fondant. I used an "I" letter cutter, but you can use the tip of a sharp paring knife; make sure the slot is large enough to fit a chocolate coin.

18 **Make the piggy parts:** Take 12 ounces of the remaining pink fondant and knead in ½ teaspoon CMC. This will be used to make the legs, ears, and tail.

19 **Make the legs:** Roll out some of the pink fondant–CMC mixture into a log that is about 6 inches long and 2 inches thick. Cut it into four equal pieces, each about 1½ inches long. Working with one leg at a time, trim the piece at an angle on top so it will tuck under the sides of the pig. You may need to keep trimming to make the leg fit, so be patient. Glue it in place with a little bit of piping gel. Repeat with the remaining legs.

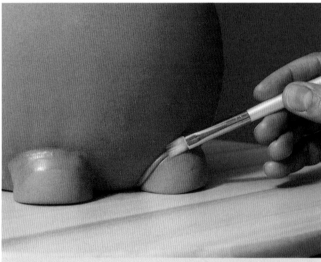

20 There will be gaps above each leg that you will need to fill in order to make them appear more seamless. Roll out four thin cords of pink fondant mixture the same length as the gaps and insert them into the gaps, securing them with a bit of water. Use a damp paintbrush to repeatedly smooth the cord, turning it into a putty that fills the gap and creating a smooth, ceramic-looking seam.

> What's most important here is that the ears are the same size and proportional to the rest of the pig.

21 **Make the ears:** Divide 2 ounces of the pink fondant–CMC mixture in half to form two equal balls. Shape each ball into a triangular shape. Using your fingers, taper the thickness of the two top sides, leaving the triangle thicker in the middle and at the bottom edge. Adjust the curve of the bottom edge so it fits snugly on the piggy's head. Now lay each ear on a rolling pin to set.

22 **Make the tail:** Roll a cord of the pink fondant–CMC mixture, and make it pointed at one end. Coil it up on itself, like a pig's curly tail, so that the pointed end is pointing up.

23 **Make the eyes:** On the nonstick surface and using the nonstick rolling pin, thinly roll out the white gum paste, then cut out two circles with a #807 piping tip. Roll the cel stick back and forth over the small circles to make them more oval shaped. For the pupils, thinly roll out some of the remaining black fondant and cut out two circles with the same piping tip. Glue the black pupils onto the white ovals using piping gel, keeping in mind the expression you want the pig to have—mine is looking up, but yours could be looking to one side, or just straight.

24 **Add the details to the pig:** Secure the tail to the pig's body with a piece of spaghetti. Attach the ears with spaghetti as well, making sure to place them evenly on either side of the head. Fill in the gaps around the ears the same way you did with the legs (see step 19).

You won't be too heartbroken when you break this bank!

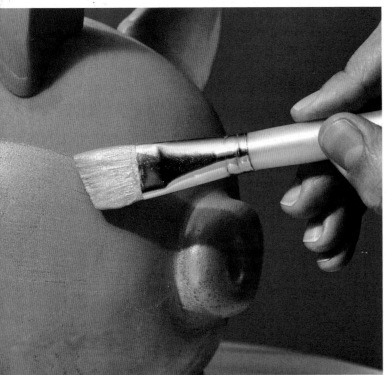

26 Unwrap the chocolate coins (I used Canadian toonies!) and paint the surfaces with silver and/or gold luster dust. Cut a small sliver off one end of one coin to make that side flat and position it in the coin slot, as if it were being dropped in. If it doesn't stay upright, carefully push it into the cake. Arrange the other coins around the piggy bank.

25 In a bowl, mix pink and pearl luster dusts (about 1 jar pink and ½ jar pearl) with enough clear food-grade alcohol to make a paint-like consistency. Use a soft paintbrush to paint the entire pig, making sure your brushstrokes are always in the same direction to give it a nice porcelain sheen. If you feel your piggy needs a second coat, allow the first coat to dry fully before applying another.

Coconut Drink

2

CAKE IT UP A NOTCH

This book has been a dream of mine for longer than I can remember, and since I'm a very sentimental person, its pages are filled with little personal tributes to the people and things I love most. This Coconut Drink cake is dedicated to my mom and the island she's from, Grenada. Grenada is a small island in the Caribbean and a very special place I hold close to my heart. Mr. Cake and I even got married there!

I chose to make a coconut cake to represent Grenada because the island is covered with palm trees and coconuts. A lot of people tell me they don't like the taste of coconut, but my coconut cake recipe always wins them over. It has a subtle yet delicious natural flavor and a moist crumb. I've even had some die-hard chocolate lovers choose my coconut cake over my chocolate cake, which says a lot! The fun of this cake is that it's literally a coconut cake—inside and out. Like my Sand Pail cake, it's the perfect cake to make for the beach lovers in your life or to bring some summer vibes to an off-season shindig. It's like caking a trip to the islands!

Coconut Drink

2

CAKE IT UP A NOTCH

⚔ Tools

6-inch round cake pan (3 inches deep)

4 (7-inch) round cake pans (3 inches deep)

Sir Squeeze-A-Lot bottle (see page 52)

Bamboo skewer

Serrated knife

Ruler and fabric measuring tape

12-inch round cake drum

Small offset spatula

2½-inch circle cutter

Paintbrushes

Rolling pins: wooden and French

🧺 Ingredients

For the coconut

1½ recipes	Yo's Coconut Cake batter (page 28)
½ recipe	Yo's Italian Meringue Buttercream (page 30)
1 (15-ounce) can	cream of coconut (such as Coco López)
1 recipe	Yo's Simple Syrup (page 34)
2½ pounds	white fondant
	Gel food colorings: off-white, black, avocado, electric green, leaf green, and crimson
4 ounces	white compound chocolate
	Confectioners' sugar for rolling fondant
	Pure vanilla extract
	Clear food-grade alcohol
	Ground allspice

For the straw

4 ounces	gum paste
	Teal gel food coloring
	Clear piping gel
	Vegetable shortening (if needed)

Day 1: Prep It

1. Preheat the oven to 350°F. Line the bottoms of one 6-inch round cake pan and four 7-inch round cake pans with parchment paper (see "How to Bake a Cake" on page 44).

2. Prepare the cake batter according to the recipe. Scrape the batter into the prepared pans and spread so that it is smooth in the pans. Bake for 1 hour 15 minutes, or until a toothpick inserted in the center comes out clean, rotating the pans halfway through. Transfer to wire racks and let cool completely in the pans. Cover tightly with plastic wrap and refrigerate overnight.

3. Prepare the buttercream according to the recipe. Add 1 cup of the cream of coconut and beat until incorporated. Cover the bowl tightly with plastic wrap and refrigerate.

4. Prepare the simple syrup according to the recipe. Let cool to room temperature. Pour into your Sir Squeeze-A-Lot bottle and refrigerate.

5. **Color 8 ounces of the white fondant off-white:** Start by kneading in a tiny bit of off-white and black food coloring, continuing to add more until the fondant is off-white.

6. Color the remaining fondant to look like the green skin of a fresh coconut by kneading in a little of each green food coloring until the color matches the real thing. If you don't have a live model or color swatch, look at photos and experiment with matching the colors. If the green is too bright, add a few specks of crimson food coloring to slightly dull it. Wrap the off-white and green fondants tightly in plastic wrap and set aside in a cool, dry place.

7. **Make the straw:** Color half of the gum paste teal (or your favorite color). Roll it into a cord about 12 inches long and ⅛ inch thick. Roll the remaining white gum paste into a cord the same size. Coat the top half of a bamboo skewer with piping gel. With both cords side by side, twist them snugly around the skewer with no gaps in between them, working quickly so the gum paste doesn't crack. (If the gum paste is drying too quickly, unroll it, separate the two colors, soften the gum paste by kneading in a little vegetable shortening, and start over.) When the cords are completely wrapped around the skewer, roll the skewer on the work surface to smooth the gum paste all around, then trim the top so that it is flat. Set aside to dry overnight.

Day 2: Cake It

1 Remove the buttercream from the fridge and let it come to room temperature. This may take a few hours.

2 Remove the cakes from the pans and peel off the parchment. Set the cakes right side up, and level them using a serrated knife and ruler (see page 48). Flip the cakes over and remove the caramelization from the bottoms using the same technique.

3 Lay out all the cakes on a clean work surface and shower them with simple syrup. Let the syrup soak in fully before continuing.

4 On a 12-inch round cake drum, stack and fill the 7-inch cakes, spreading a dollop of coconut buttercream over each layer with a small offset spatula and ending with the 6-inch layer on top. (Do not spread buttercream on the top layer.) Transfer to the fridge to chill for 20 to 30 minutes, until the buttercream is firm to the touch.

6 **Create a hollow at the top of the coconut:** Make a circle indentation using a 2½-inch circle cutter, then use a spoon to scoop out a hole. (Yay! A snack!) Scoop no deeper than two cake layers.

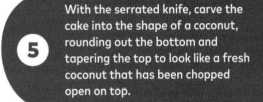

5 With the serrated knife, carve the cake into the shape of a coconut, rounding out the bottom and tapering the top to look like a fresh coconut that has been chopped open on top.

7 Use a small offset spatula to crumb coat the cake with some of the buttercream (see page 56). Transfer to the fridge to chill for 20 to 30 minutes, until the crumb coat is firm to the touch.

8 In a stainless steel bowl set over a pan of lightly simmering water, melt the compound chocolate, stirring until smooth. Pour some into the hollow in the top of the cake. Before it firms up, use a paintbrush—using upward brushstrokes only—to coat the exposed cake inside the hole with the white chocolate so the cake won't dry out.

9 Apply another layer of buttercream over the crumb coat, trying to get it as smooth as possible. Return it to the fridge for another 20 to 30 minutes, until the buttercream is firm to the touch.

10 Measure the top part of the coconut, from the midway point (where the taper begins) up and over to the other side. Dust the work surface with confectioners' sugar and, using a wooden rolling pin, roll out the off-white fondant to that size and ⅛ inch thick. Try not to handle the fondant too much—use the rolling pin to move it instead of your hands. Pick up the pin, then quickly and carefully cover the top of the cake with the fondant, smoothing as you go. Use the circle cutter to cut away the excess where the hollow is at the top of the cake.

11 This off-white fondant only covers the top third of the coconut, so trim the fondant where the tapered top part of the coconut meets the rounded bottom part. Put the cake in the fridge to chill for about 20 minutes, until the fondant is firm.

It's much easier to score chilled fondant than soft fondant, so refrigerate as needed.

12 To make the top of the coconut appear more lifelike and fibrous, cut shallow score marks in the off-white fondant with the tip of a paring knife in a downward motion.

13 Measure the whole cake, from the base of one side, over the top, to the base of the other side. Roll out the green fondant ⅛ inch thick to be a little larger than the size you'll need. Set a French rolling pin in the center of the fondant and fold one end up over it. Try not to handle the fondant too much. Pick up the pin, then quickly and carefully drape the fondant over the cake, then smooth it along the bottom half of the cake only, using your hands. With the paring knife, trim any excess from the bottom.

14 Tear away the top part of the green fondant until it's close to where the off-white fondant ends. Use the paring knife to trim away the green fondant so there is a clean seam between both colors. Don't worry too much about the line being perfectly straight.

15 Use your fingertips to gently smooth the green fondant into the off-white fondant. Put the cake in the fridge to chill for about 20 minutes, until the fondant is firm.

16 With the tip and sharp edge of the paring knife, give the green part of your coconut little nicks, bumps, and scratches like a real coconut. Adding lifelike details like this will really take your cake to the next level.

17 Time to paint! Paint the off-white portion of the cake with vanilla, using up-and-down brushstrokes. Mix off-white food coloring with clear food-grade alcohol and paint inside the rim of the hollow in the top to make it look as though the coconut has oxidized.

18 For the green part, mix electric green food coloring into the off-white and alcohol mixture. Brush it onto the green fondant using up-and-down brushstrokes to give the green color a more realistic look. Let the paint dry fully before proceeding.

> This cake is dedicated to my mom's Grenadian roots, but on my YouTube channel I've caked in honor of my dad's German heritage, too—an Oktoberfest Frankfurter cake!

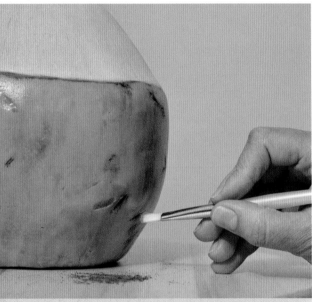

19 Using a dry paintbrush, dab allspice onto the nicks and scratches of the green portion of the coconut. Use a little more vanilla to darken along the border of the green and white parts.

20 Before serving, for a realistic effect, pour some of the remaining cream of coconut into the hollow in the top of the coconut. Don't worry—the white chocolate coating will prevent the cream of coconut from making the cake soggy!

21 Finish by inserting the gum paste straw into the cake and sticking in a paper umbrella or little flag like my Grenada one. Cheers!

Golden Pyramid

2

CAKE IT UP A NOTCH

SERVES 16 TO 20

Most of the novelty cakes I make involve fondant, because when it comes to creating custom, lifelike cake details, fondant is king. But since this cake was inspired by the ancient golden pyramids, I thought it would be best to enshrine it with age-old ingredients and historical materials like chocolate and gold. For chocolate lovers like me, this cake is basically a wonder of the world, but you could cover it with other types of candy. I once covered a giant pyramid cake with (LOTS) of gummies on my YouTube channel.

The real treasure of this cake is its secret chamber filled with chocolate coins. Everyone loves a cake with a surprise inside, but this one is extra fun because it plays to the theme. I always say baking is a science, but this cake will definitely make history. You won't wanna wait to put it in ruins!

Golden Pyramid

2

CAKE IT UP A NOTCH

Tools

2 (4-inch) square cake pans (3 inches deep)

2 (6-inch) square cake pans (3 inches deep)

2 (8-inch) square cake pans (3 inches deep)

Sir Squeeze-A-Lot bottle (see page 52)

Serrated knife

Ruler

14-inch square cake drum

Piping bag

#809 round piping tip

Small offset spatula

Soft-bristled brush

I used a brand-new makeup brush

Ingredients

2 recipes	Yo's Ultimate Vanilla Cake batter (page 24)
1 cup	chocolate sprinkles
2 recipes	Yo's Dark Chocolate Ganache (page 36)
2 recipes	Yo's Simple Syrup (page 34)
4 dozen	gold-foil-wrapped chocolate coins (more or fewer, depending on size)
8 pounds	chocolate rectangles (such as Hershey's chocolate nuggets)
4 (2.5 gram) jars	gold luster dust
	Golden sugar crystals (optional)

Day 1: Prep It

1 Preheat the oven to 350°F. Line the bottoms of two 4-inch, two 6-inch, and two 8-inch square cake pans with parchment paper (see "How to Bake a Cake" on page 44).

2 Prepare the cake batter according to the recipe. Gently fold in the sprinkles. (Add the sprinkles just before baking, so they don't bleed and muddle the color of the cake.) Scrape the batter into the prepared pans, filling each pan a little less than half full, and spread so that it is smooth in the pans. Bake for 30 to 45 minutes, or until a toothpick inserted in the center comes out clean, rotating the pans halfway through. The smallest cake will take the shortest time, the largest the longest. Transfer to wire racks and let cool completely in the pans. Cover tightly with plastic wrap and refrigerate overnight.

3 Prepare the ganache according to the recipe. Let cool completely at room temperature, then cover and set aside.

4 Prepare the simple syrup according to the recipe. Let cool to room temperature. Pour into your Sir Squeeze-A-Lot bottle and refrigerate.

Day 2: Cake It

1 Remove the cakes from the pans and peel off the parchment. Set the cakes right side up, and level them using a serrated knife and ruler (see page 48). Flip the cakes over and remove the caramelization from the bottoms using the same technique. Make sure all the cakes are the same height.

2 It's time to start creating secret chambers for your chocolate treasure! Lay out four chocolate coins in a square arrangement, and measure the length and width of that square. From a piece of paper, cut out a square template that's the size of that square. Place the template precisely in the center of an 8-inch layer of cake. Use a sharp paring knife to cut the square out of the cake. Repeat on the second 8-inch cake. Reserve the cut-out squares, as they will become the two top layers of your pyramid.

3 Create another square paper template that is the size of a single coin. Place the template precisely in the center of a 6-inch square cake. Use a sharp paring knife to cut the square out of the cake. Repeat on the second 6-inch cake. (Enjoy these smaller cut-outs as a snack!)

4 Lay out all the cakes, including the two cut-out squares, on a clean work surface and shower them with simple syrup. Let the syrup soak in fully before continuing.

5 Place an 8-inch square cake layer on a 14-inch square cake drum. Transfer the ganache to a piping bag fitted with a #809 round tip and pipe a layer of ganache on the top surface of the cake. Spread it with a small offset spatula, trying your best to keep the ganache out of the inner square (the secret chamber).

6 Top with the second 8-inch square cake, scraping away any ganache that seeps into the chamber. Fill the chamber with four stacks of coins, stacking until they're level with the top of the cake layer.

7 Pipe and spread ganache on the top, leaving a 1-inch border of uncovered cake around the outside edges, then top with a 6-inch cake, centering it over the 8-inch layers. Pipe and spread ganache over the top of the 6-inch cake, avoiding the chamber, and top with the second 6-inch cake. Fill the chamber with a stack of coins.

8 Pipe and spread ganache on the top, leaving a 1-inch border, and center a 4-inch cake on top. Pipe and spread ganache over it, then top with the second 4-inch cake. Pipe and spread ganache over the entire top.

9 Center one of the cut-out square cake pieces on top and spread ganache on top. Top with the second cut-out square (but do not spread ganache on the top). Transfer the cake to the fridge to chill for 20 to 30 minutes, until the ganache is firm to the touch.

11 With the serrated knife, cut two sides of the pyramid, cutting slowly and following the diagonal lines you made on both sides of the cake. Make sure the knife cuts right through to the other side. This will leave you with a cake that has two A-line sides and two sides that are still terraced. Use the same technique as you did for the first two sides to cut a diagonal line down each terraced side, leaving you with a pyramid shape.

10 Time to carve the pyramid! Measure and find the center of the top layer and mark a cross in the top of the cake. With one side of the cake facing you, on the left corner of the cake, hold a ruler from the mark on the top diagonally down to the bottom edge of the cake. With a paring knife, mark a diagonal line down the cake. Repeat on the right corner. Turn the cake front to back and repeat on the other two corners.

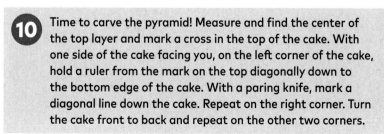

12 Use the small offset spatula to crumb coat the entire cake with ganache (see page 56). If the ganache is becoming too firm to spread, gently reheat it in the microwave for no more than 10 seconds at a time until more spreadable, stirring in between. Transfer the cake to the fridge to chill for 20 to 30 minutes, until the ganache is firm to the touch.

13 To add the chocolates, you'll need to ice only part of the cake at a time, attaching the chocolates as you go. Starting at the base of the pyramid, ice the cake with ganache about 1 inch up the sides of the pyramid and all the way around the base. Working quickly while the ganache is still soft, add the chocolates, placing them at the corners first and building inward until they meet in the center of each side.

> Work fast with the ganache so that it doesn't firm up too soon. If you feel you need more time, add chocolates to only one side of the pyramid at a time.

14 If they don't meet in the center of each side, trim the chocolates with a sharp paring knife to fill in the gaps, making sure that the partial chocolates don't all end up in the same place on each row.

15 Repeat icing the sides about an inch at a time and placing the chocolates, building up to the top of the pyramid.

16 Once the cake is covered in chocolate rectangles, use a soft-bristled brush to brush gold luster dust all over the chocolate rectangles. The luster will adhere perfectly to the chocolate, and the soft brush will ensure that there are no visible brushstrokes and give it a nice sheen.

17 If you like, pile golden sugar "sand" around the base of the pyramid. To complete the look, dust any leftover chocolate rectangles with gold and arrange them off to the side to look like ancient rubble. Now dig in to enjoy your buried treasure!

Mega Chocolate Bar

In my early caking days, I ran a small custom cake business where this cake was a popular choice for birthdays, bat/bar mitzvahs, and other occasions. I love this cake because it's so versatile and fun to personalize. You can completely customize the wrapper for the person you're making it for by incorporating their name, preferred colors, and even their age or birthdate as the chocolate's weight.

For this cake, we had so much fun creating our own original Cake It bar, and worked with my best friend, Bianca, who is a graphic designer, to design the wrapper. If you want to recreate the wrapper of your favorite candy bar, print out an enlarged version of the logo and use it as a template. The designing doesn't stop at the wrapper, though—you can customize the imprint on the bar itself, creating lines or patterns or imprinting the bar's name onto it. Another way to tailor this cake is to replace the wafer cookie layer inside with a favorite chocolate bar. So if you like creating personal touches like I do, and are looking to serve up a real crowd-pleaser at your next celebration, you'll definitely want to sink your teeth into this one!

Mega Chocolate Bar

2

CAKE IT UP A NOTCH

Tools

9 × 13-inch cake pan (3 inches deep)

Sir Squeeze-A-Lot bottle (see page 52)

Nonstick mat or board

Rolling pins: small nonstick, wooden, and French

A few sheets of paper

Serrated knife

Ruler and fabric measuring tape

14 × 19-inch cake drum

Small offset spatula

Fondant smoother

Ball sculpting tool or letter cutters

Veining sculpting tool

Paintbrushes

Paper logo template

X-Acto knife

#9 round piping tip

2½-inch circle cutter (optional)

Ingredients

1½ recipes	Yo's Ultimate Chocolate Cake batter (page 22)
2 recipes	Yo's Dark Chocolate Ganache (page 36)
1 recipe	Yo's Chocolate Swiss Meringue Buttercream (page 32)
1 recipe	Yo's Simple Syrup (page 34)
8 ounces	gum paste
1 pound	white fondant
3 ounces	black fondant
About 48	sugar wafer cookies (you'll need about two 14-ounce packs)
	Confectioners' sugar for rolling fondant
1 pound	chocolate fondant
	Corn starch
	Silver luster dust
	Clear food-grade alcohol
2 pounds	yellow fondant
4 ounces	purple fondant
	Clear piping gel

Day 1: Prep It

1 Preheat the oven to 350°F. Line the bottom of a 9 × 13-inch cake pan with parchment paper (see "How to Bake a Cake" on page 44).

2 Prepare the cake batter according to the recipe. Pour the batter into the prepared pan. Bake for 1 hour 10 minutes, or until a toothpick inserted in the center comes out clean, rotating the pan halfway through. Transfer to a wire rack and let cool completely in the pan. Cover tightly with plastic wrap and refrigerate overnight.

3 Prepare the ganache according to the recipe. Let cool completely at room temperature, then cover and set aside overnight.

4 Prepare the buttercream according to the recipe. Cover the bowl tightly with plastic wrap and refrigerate.

5 Prepare the simple syrup according to the recipe. Let cool to room temperature. Pour into your Sir Squeeze-A-Lot bottle and refrigerate.

6 **For the foil wrapper, make 50/50:** Knead together the gum paste, 8 ounces white fondant, and ½ ounce black fondant. This mixture, called "50/50," is stronger than fondant and not as quick to dry out as gum paste. Divide into two pieces.

7 Divide one piece of the 50/50 into three to five smaller pieces. On a nonstick mat or board, using a small nonstick rolling pin, roll out no more than half of the 50/50 as thinly as you can—I'm talking paper thin. This will become the foil that is torn away from the chocolate bar. Rip the sides of the rolled-out 50/50; don't cut it with a knife, but use your hands so the ends look torn. Crumple up a few sheets of paper and drape the ripped pieces of 50/50 over the crumpled paper. Set aside to dry overnight. Tightly wrap the remaining 50/50 in plastic wrap and set aside.

Day 2: Cake It

1 Remove the buttercream from the fridge and let it come to room temperature. This may take a few hours.

2 Remove the cake from the pan and peel off the parchment. Set the cake right side up, and level it using a serrated knife and ruler (see page 48). Save the hump, because you will use it later.

3 Use the serrated knife to trim 2 inches off one long side of the cake to make a 7 × 13-inch rectangle. Cut that rectangle in half horizontally to make two 7 × 13-inch layers.

4 Level the reserved cake hump to the same height as one of the 7 × 13-inch cake layers. From the leveled hump, cut a 7 × 8-inch rectangle (and snack on the trimmings!). Cut that rectangle in half to make two 7 × 4-inch rectangles. Stack these two rectangles on top of each other and set the stack beside the short end of the 7 × 13-inch layered cake so that you have a 7 × 17-inch slab.

5 Mark ½ inch in from the top edge on all four sides, then cut on a slant from the ½-inch mark down to the bottom outer edge on all four sides to create tapered edges.

6 Lay out all the cake pieces on a clean work surface and shower them with simple syrup. Let the syrup soak in fully before continuing.

7 Arrange the bottom cake layers (large rectangle plus a small rectangle on the end) on a cake drum. Using a small offset spatula, spread some buttercream on the bottom layer. Cover the entire surface with wafer cookies, lining them up in rows with no space between them and trimming cookies to fit as needed. Spread another layer of buttercream on top of the cookies, then add the top layers of the cake. If needed, trim the angled cuts on the sides of the cake so they line up.

8 Use the offset spatula to crumb coat the cake with some of the ganache (see page 56). Transfer to the fridge to chill for 20 to 30 minutes, until the ganache is firm to the touch.

9 Using the offset or a straight spatula, apply the remaining ganache over the crumb coat. Return it to the fridge for another 20 to 30 minutes, until the ganache is firm to the touch.

10 Create the end of the chocolate bar: Dust the work surface with confectioners' sugar and, using a wooden rolling pin, roll out the chocolate fondant until ¼ inch thick and large enough to cover about 3½ inches in from the end of the cake and fully cover the two corners at that end. Set a French rolling pin in the center of the fondant and fold one end up over it. Try not to handle the fondant too much. Pick up the pin, then quickly and carefully drape the fondant over one end of the chocolate bar. Smooth the fondant with a fondant smoother, then trim away any excess fondant from the base with a paring knife. Using a ruler and a knife, cut a clean line in the fondant—this is the edge where the yellow wrapper will meet it later.

11 Customize the chocolate bar by using letter cutters to imprint the name of the chocolate bar (like I did) or the name of the person you're making the cake for. Use a measuring tape to help you line up your cutters and make your imprint straight and centered. Dust the letters in corn starch for a clean imprint. You can also create a pattern on your fondant with a sculpting tool or score it with a paring knife.

12 Create the foil end: Roll out the reserved gray 50/50 thinner than ⅛ inch. You'll be using this to cover ½ inch of the other end of your cake. Drape it over the bare end of the chocolate bar (opposite the chocolate end). Smooth it out with a fondant smoother, then trim away any excess 50/50 with a paring knife. Using the ruler and the paring knife, cut away the gray 50/50 to create a clean line on the top and sides of the cake.

13 To make the folded foil wrapper corners, make a small mark on the bottom edge of the end 2½ inches in from each corner. Using a veining tool and a ruler as a guide, imprint a line diagonally from that mark to the top corner so that it looks like a fold in the foil.

14 In a small bowl, mix silver luster dust with enough clear food-grade alcohol to make a paint-like consistency. Paint the foil on the end of the chocolate bar and all the crumpled pieces of 50/50 with the silver luster paint. When painting the crumpled pieces, be sure to handle them carefully, as they are thin and fragile. If they do happen to break, not to worry: they'll just look like smaller pieces of the foil wrapper. Set aside to dry.

15 Once the silver paint is fully dry, measure the entire length of the cake (including the foil end and the fondant end) and the width from the base of one side, over the top, and down to the base of the other side. Roll out yellow fondant a little larger than this size and ⅛ inch thick. Cover the cake with it. Trim the two long sides at the base to be flush with the cake drum. Cut a straight line where the yellow fondant meets the foil and remove any excess.

16 Create the torn wrapper: At the chocolate fondant end, cut an uneven edge diagonally across the yellow fondant, being careful not to cut down into the chocolate layer. Slide a piece of paper or a thin piece of cardboard underneath the yellow fondant before you cut so you don't cut into the chocolate layer, then slip the paper out. Gently fold the yellow fondant back to look like a chocolate bar that's been unwrapped.

17 Time to have fun with the label! Create a paper template using a font that screams classic candy bar, and use it to cut out letters from purple and white fondant with an X-Acto knife. I recommend doing your lettering in two layers of contrasting colors, one larger than the other, so that the letters will be outlined—this will make the logo really pop.

Now you can have yo' cake and eat it too!

19 Apply all the fondant logo pieces and letters to the cake using piping gel.

20 Style the crumpled foil wrappers around the "torn wrapper" end of the cake for a realistic effect.

18 **Add black fondant details:** I made a slogan that says, "Have yo' cake & eat it too!" using letter cutters and a #9 round piping tip for the dot on the exclamation point, but you could add "Happy Birthday!" and the chocolate bar "weight" (I sometimes use the person's age or birth date as the weight if I'm making this as a birthday cake) or whatever personalized message or designs you'd like.

21 Roll out a piece of yellow fondant, and cut a rough triangle that looks like a torn piece of wrapper. Roll out purple fondant very thinly and use letter cutters to cut out the numbers for the candy bar "weight." (I used my birthday!) Attach them to the torn piece of wrapper with piping gel and artfully crumple the fondant.

You can go one step further and use a circle cutter to create a bite out of the cake to reveal the yummy sugar wafer layer inside.

Purse

Early on in my caking career, I caked a designer purse that ended up being featured in a fashion magazine. It was so exciting to see one of my cake creations in print for the first time ever. If I only knew then that all these years later I'd have a whole book full of them!

SERVES 8 TO 10

Given the history, I obviously had to make sure a purse cake made it into these pages, although this one is more of a clutch. I love clutches, especially vintage ones because they often have a lovely lining. Those linings were the inspiration for using Pink Velvet inside this cake. Get it?

Have fun playing fashion designer! You can experiment with colors, patterns, and even stitching details to create your own design. But be careful, there is one big challenge with this cake—trying not to be disappointed that it isn't real. I loved my clutch cake design so much, I was sad I couldn't actually carry it around. I mean, how great would this clutch look with a cake tee?

Purse

2

**CAKE IT
UP A
NOTCH**

Tools

11 × 15-inch cake pan (3 inches deep)

Sir Squeeze-A-Lot bottle (see page 52)

Toothpicks

Serrated knife

Ruler and fabric measuring tape

12-inch square cake drum

Small offset spatula

Rolling pins: wooden, French, and small nonstick

4 paintbrushes (similar size and shape)

Clay extruder with round faceplate

Overstitch wheel

Nonstick mat or board

#7 round piping tip

Ingredients

1½ recipes	Yo's Pink Velvet Cake batter (page 26)
½ recipe	Yo's Italian Meringue Buttercream (page 30)
½ recipe	Yo's Simple Syrup (page 34)
4 ounces	gum paste
	Gel food colorings: lemon yellow, white, pink, turquoise, and black
2	large yellow gumballs (plus a few extras in case of mistakes)
	Gold luster dust
	Clear food-grade alcohol
	Confectioners' sugar for rolling fondant
2½ pounds	white fondant
	Vegetable shortening
4 ounces	pink fondant
	Clear piping gel

Day 1: Prep It

1 Preheat the oven to 350°F. Line an 11 × 15-inch cake pan with parchment paper (see "How to Bake a Cake" on page 44).

2 Prepare the cake batter according to the recipe. Scrape it into the prepared pan and spread so that it is smooth in the pan. Bake for 1 hour 15 minutes, or until a toothpick inserted in the center comes out clean, rotating the pan halfway through. Transfer to a wire rack and let cool completely in the pan. Cover tightly with plastic wrap and refrigerate overnight.

3 Prepare the buttercream according to the recipe. Cover the bowl tightly with plastic wrap and refrigerate.

4 Prepare the simple syrup according to the recipe. Let cool to room temperature. Pour into your Sir Squeeze-A-Lot bottle and refrigerate.

5 Dye the gum paste by kneading in lemon yellow food coloring. Roll into a ball, wrap tightly with plastic wrap, and set aside in a cool, dry place.

6 **Paint the gumballs:** Find the flattest side of each gumball and poke a small hole in it with a toothpick, being careful not to poke through the other end. Remove the toothpick. In a small bowl, dilute some of the gold luster with clear food-grade alcohol, adding the alcohol a little at a time until you get a paint-like consistency. Place a gumball in the bowl, and swirl it around until coated. Avoid touching the gumball with your hands; tip it out of the bowl onto a clean surface to dry. Repeat to coat the second gumball, and do a few extras in case of breakage. Let the leftover paint dry in the bowl; you will use the luster again later to paint the clasp.

Day 2: Cake It

① Remove the buttercream from the fridge and let it come to room temperature. This may take a few hours.

② Remove the cake from the pan and peel off the parchment. Set the cake right side up, and level it using a serrated knife and ruler (see page 48). Flip the cake over and remove the caramelization from the bottom using the same technique, then trim the caramelization from the sides.

④ Lay out all the rectangles on a clean work surface and shower them with simple syrup. Let the syrup soak in fully before proceeding.

⑤ On a 12-inch square cake drum, stack and fill the cake layers, starting with the 4-inch-wide rectangle on the bottom and ending with the 1-inch-wide rectangle on the top. Spread some of the buttercream over each layer with a small offset spatula, and center each layer on top of the previous one. (Do not spread buttercream on the top cake layer.) Chill for 20 to 30 minutes, until the buttercream is firm to the touch.

③ Using the ruler and serrated knife, cut the cake into five rectangles, each 11 inches long and of graduated widths: 4 inches, 3½ inches, 3 inches, 2½ inches, and 1 inch.

⑥ Using the serrated knife, carve the cake into a soft, rounded A-line shape on the back and front as well as the ends. Carve indents into each end of the cake where there would be a natural fold or pleat in the purse fabric.

7 Use the offset spatula to crumb coat the cake with some of the buttercream (see page 56). Transfer to the fridge to chill for 20 to 30 minutes, until the crumb coat is firm to the touch.

8 Apply another layer of buttercream over the crumb coat, trying to get it as smooth as possible. Return it to the fridge for 20 to 30 minutes, until the buttercream is firm to the touch.

9 **Cover the end panels of the purse with white fondant:** Dust the work surface with confectioners' sugar. Using a wooden rolling pin, for each end panel, roll out 4 ounces of the white fondant until ¼ inch thick. Apply the fondant to each end of the cake, using your fingers to smooth it into the natural fold you created. With a sharp paring knife, trim the excess fondant from the bottom and top. Now trim the excess from each end, but leave a slight overlap so the end panels can wrap around onto the front and back just a bit, like fabric would. Make sure you trim both end panels the same, so that the bag looks even and symmetrical.

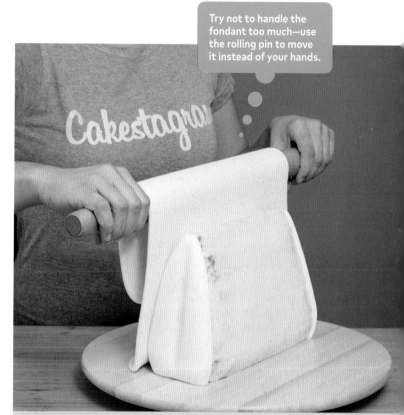

Try not to handle the fondant too much—use the rolling pin to move it instead of your hands.

Cakestagram

10 **Cover the front and back of the purse with white fondant:** Measure the width of the cake from the base of the front, over the top, to the base of the back. Roll out a sheet of white fondant until it is a little larger than the needed size. Set a French rolling pin in the center of the fondant and fold one end up over it. Pick up the pin, then quickly and carefully drape the fondant over the cake from front to back. With your hands, smooth the fondant into the curves of the purse.

Cake It Up a Notch   **193**

11 Tuck and press the excess fondant toward the underside of the cake, then trim away any excess with the paring knife. It can be helpful to hold your knife at a slight angle when trimming here. Trim the excess fondant from each side of the purse where the fondant meets the side panels.

12 **Take a measurement for the clasp:** Measure from the center of one side panel, up over the top of the cake, and down to the center of the other side panel. Jot it down!

You measure the cake before painting to avoid smudges.

13 **Prepare "paints" in four separate small bowls:** Put ½ teaspoon white food coloring in each bowl, then add small amounts of coloring to the bowls until you're happy with the hue as follows: yellow, pink, turquoise, and black. For black, you'll want to add more food coloring, as the white can make it look more light gray. Stir each thoroughly until you achieve a consistent color.

14 It's time to paint! I chose a simple pattern that consists of light downward brushstrokes. Using a set of four similar paintbrushes, begin to paint on your pattern, starting with the lightest color and moving on to the darkest. I started with yellow paint and applied random downward brushstrokes over all four sides of the purse, then moved on to pink, turquoise, and finally black. Have fun experimenting with the patterns—depending on your comfort level, you can try anything from animal prints to polka dots!

15 Transfer the cake to the fridge to chill for about 1 hour to dry somewhat. Remember that the paint will never fully dry, so always be careful handling the painted cake.

16 Make the cord details for the sides of the purse: Knead a little shortening into the pink fondant to soften it, then roll the fondant into a cord. Push the cord through a clay extruder fitted with a round faceplate. Using piping gel, attach the cord to the purse, starting at the base of the front on one side and moving up and around to the base of the back. Repeat on the other side.

17 Add the stitch details: Carefully run an overstitch wheel alongside the cording on each side of the purse, then across the base of the front and back panels. This will make it look like the fabric panels were sewn together.

18 Make the gum paste clasp: Check the measurement you jotted down earlier. On a nonstick mat or board, using a small nonstick rolling pin, roll out the yellow gum paste until ⅛ inch thick and slightly longer than the length you noted. Cut two ½-inch-wide strips and glue them on top of one another with piping gel. Pick up the bands so that the seam is upright and lay it—don't press it yet—across the top of the purse and down the sides, gluing it on with a bit of piping gel.

> Gum paste is meant to set up fast. You'll need to work quickly so it doesn't crack before you're finished. If you find that the gum paste is drying out as you work, just reknead it with a little more shortening and try again.

19 Trim the ends of the clasp with a sharp pairing knife so they extend the same distance down each side of the purse. Now press the clasp onto the cake. Use your knife to accentuate the seam a little where the two halves of the clasp would meet. Use a #7 round piping tip to create an indent at each end of the clasp, on both the front and back.

> Of course I have a watermelon purse. It was a gift from Walter!

20 Now it's time to paint the clasp. Reconstitute the reserved gold luster in the bowl by adding more alcohol. With a clean brush, paint the clasp with the gold luster paint. Take your time doing this—painting details directly on a cake is always tricky. Allow the luster paint to dry before proceeding—depending on the thickness of the paint, this should take about 30 minutes.

> If you add too much alcohol and find your paint is too thin, you can either add more luster to thicken it or wait until the alcohol starts to evaporate.

21 **Add two gumballs:** Insert two toothpicks into the top of the clasp, each one slightly off-center, one in the "front" clasp and one in the "back" clasp. Leave ½ inch of the toothpicks exposed. Affix the gumballs onto the toothpicks, using the holes you made before. Now your cake is ready for a night on the town!

Cake It

Cake It to the Limit

If you've made it this far, you're practically a pro! We should celebrate your incredible accomplishment— with cake, of course! Seven cakes, to be exact. In this final section, you'll find advanced projects that require more time, patience, and skill. But I believe in you and know that, like a cake in the oven, you'll rise to this next batch of caking challenges.

Some of these cakes have been on my bucket list for a while, so it was a lot of fun for me to finally cake them myself, while others are old favorites with a new twist. All of them will help you to practice new skills, such as learning how to create sharp, clean edges and sculpt more complicated shapes. You'll also be working with more dowels, gum paste, and fondant details. These cakes may look simple, but each presents some new skill or technique that will cake you to the next level.

Now that you are virtually a cake master, I encourage you to be creative and have fun. Customize some of the detailing on these cakes to make them your own.

After close to two decades of caking, I still feel so much pride and satisfaction when I see the details come together on a cake. It's always amazing to see a pile of ingredients (neatly organized, of course) turn into an incredible cake to share with my loved ones and with all my YoYos around the world. I love that magical process, and I know you will, too.

So, it's time to reach for the sky and cake it to the limit!

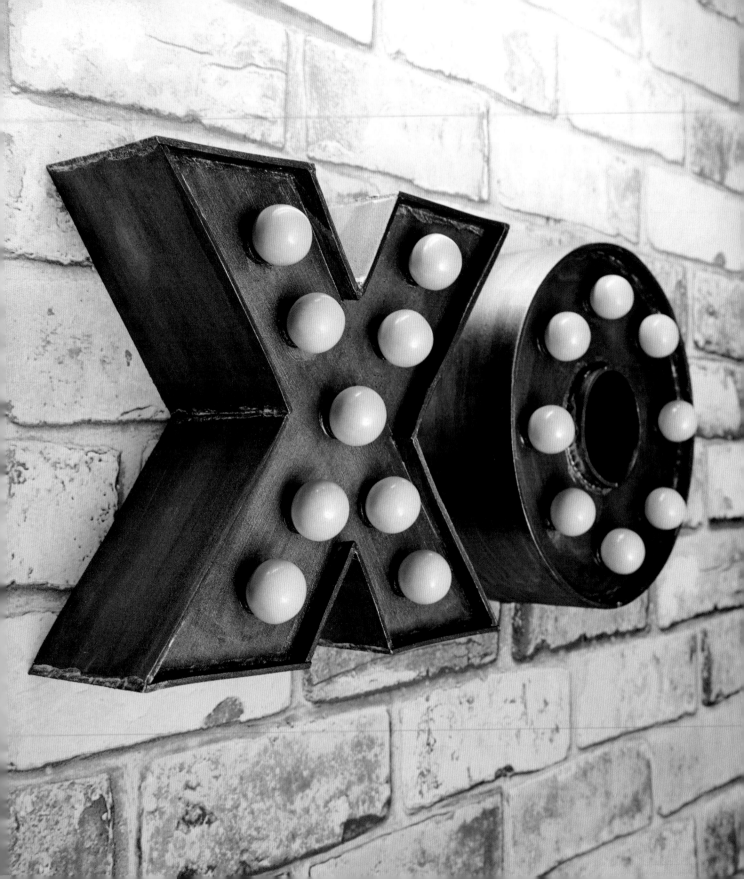

Marquee Letters

Here's something most people don't know about me: I have an obsession with fonts and typesetting. It's almost on par with my love of rulers and cake books—*almost*. For years, whenever I've come across stamps, stickers, or cut-outs of my loved ones' initials, I always buy them, so you can imagine how large my collection is today. Looking for a wooden Y to hang on the wall? I've got it. Need a G sticker for some crafting? I'm your girl.

So in honor of my font fascination *and* to answer the many requests from YoYos who've been asking me to show them how to cake letters, I present to you this XO Marquee Letter cake, glimmering like real metal and studded with gumball "lights." Originally I was going to cake a Y (of course!), but building an XO allows me to show you how to work with both a straight-edged letter and a round one—so it will give you all the techniques you need to figure out *any* letter. It's also the perfect cake for anyone you want to give edible hugs and kisses to— consider this my XO to all of you!

Marquee Letters

3

CAKE IT TO THE LIMIT

☒ Tools

7 × 11-inch cake pan (3 inches deep)	
8-inch round cake pan (3 inches deep)	
Sir Squeeze-A-Lot bottle (see page 52)	
Serrated knives (large and small)	
Ruler and fabric measuring tape	
7-inch round cake pan (to use as a template only)	
2¾-inch circle cutter	
2 (10-inch) square cake drums	
Spatulas: small offset and straight	
Rolling pins: wooden, French, and small nonstick	
2 (10-inch) square cake boards	
Fondant smoother	
Round piping tips: #805 and #809	
Paintbrushes	

🪣 Ingredients

2 recipes	Yo's Ultimate Vanilla Cake batter (page 24)
	Gel food colorings: lemon yellow and pink
½ recipe	Yo's Italian Meringue Buttercream (page 30)
1 recipe	Yo's Simple Syrup (page 34)
2 pounds	white fondant
2½ ounces	black fondant
	Confectioners' sugar for rolling fondant
2½ teaspoons	CMC powder
2 (2.5 gram) jars	silver luster dust
1 (2.5 gram) jar	black luster dust
	Clear food-grade alcohol
	Clear piping gel
17 (1-inch)	white gumballs

Day 1: Prep It

1 Preheat the oven to 350°F. Line the bottoms of a 7 × 11-inch cake pan and an 8-inch round cake pan with parchment paper (see "How to Bake a Cake" on page 44).

2 Prepare the cake batter according to the recipe. Divide the batter in half. Dye one half yellow by folding in lemon yellow food coloring until completely incorporated; dye the other half pink by folding in pink food coloring. Using a rubber spatula, dollop the batters into both pans, alternating colors. Fill each pan halfway with batter and tap gently on surface to settle the batter. There's no need to swirl; we will let them bake together naturally. Bake for 1 hour 15 minutes, or until a toothpick inserted in the center comes out clean, rotating the pans halfway through. Transfer to wire racks and let cool completely in the pans. Cover tightly with plastic wrap and refrigerate overnight.

3 Prepare the buttercream according to the recipe. Cover the bowl tightly with plastic wrap and refrigerate.

4 Prepare the simple syrup according to the recipe. Let cool to room temperature. Pour into your Sir Squeeze-A-Lot bottle and refrigerate.

5 Knead together the white fondant and black fondant to make gray, kneading until the color is uniform throughout. Wrap tightly with plastic wrap and set aside in a cool, dry place.

Day 2: Cake It

1 Remove the buttercream from the fridge and let it come to room temperature. This may take a few hours.

2 Remove the cakes from the pans and peel off the parchment. Set the cakes right side up, and level them using a serrated knife and ruler. Flip the cakes over and remove the caramelization from the bottoms using the same technique (see page 48). Remove the caramelization from the sides of the round cake by placing a 7-inch round cake pan upside-down on top of the cake and cutting with a small serrated knife straight down into the cake around the circle.

3 Using the large serrated knife and ruler, cut both cakes in two layers to make a total of four layers.

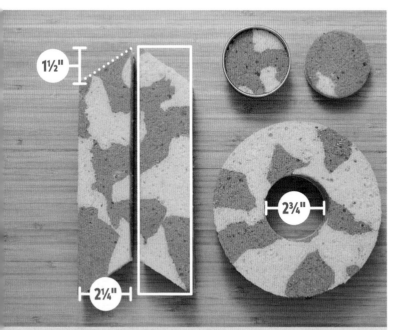

4 **For the O:** Working one layer at a time, and using a 2¾-inch circle cutter, cut a hole in the center of each round. Make sure the holes on the two cakes line up.

5 **For the X:** Stack the rectangular cake layers on top of each other. Using a ruler and serrated knife, remove caramelization from the long sides. Cut two (stacked) strips that are 2¼ inches wide and 11 inches long, avoiding the sides with the caramelization. To cut your angled end, set one strip with the narrow end closest to you and measure 1½ inches down from the far right corner; cut from the top left corner to that mark to create an angled end. At the bottom of that same strip, cut the same angle in the same direction. Repeat with the second strip of stacked cake layers, but this time cut the angled ends in the opposite direction. When the two stacked strips are arranged side by side (as pictured), they should mirror each other.

6 Arrange one stacked strip at a 45-degree angle, to make one line of the X shape. Cut the other strip in half on a 45-degree angle. Arrange the two halves against the first strip to make an X shape. This line of your X will be too long on either end. Lay your ruler on top of your strips so that it is flush with the top end of the uncut strip. Trim your half strip to match it so that it's even straight across the top. Do the same at the bottom of the X.

10 Apply another layer of buttercream over the crumb coat, making sure to keep your cakes level and the edges very sharp. Chill the cakes intermittently if needed. Return them to the fridge for 20 to 30 minutes, until the buttercream is firm to the touch.

11 Give the cakes one final ice to build up any corners and edges where needed. Return to the fridge for another 20 to 30 minutes, until the buttercream is firm to the touch.

Always be sure to place the covered side of your cake board against the cake.

7 Take apart the stacked X and O layers and lay out all the cakes on a clean work surface. Shower them with simple syrup and let the syrup soak in fully before continuing.

8 On two 10-inch square cake drums, stack and fill the X and O, spreading some buttercream over the bottom layers with a small offset spatula. Transfer to the fridge to chill for 20 to 30 minutes, until the buttercream is firm to the touch.

9 Use the offset and straight spatulas to crumb coat both cakes with some more buttercream. Transfer to the fridge to chill for 20 to 30 minutes, until the crumb coat is firm to the touch (see page 56).

For sharp edges and corners, I love using an offset spatula.

12 **Cover the top of each cake with fondant:** Measure the width of your O. Dust the work surface with confectioners' sugar and, using a wooden rolling pin, roll out gray fondant until it is ⅛ inch thick and slightly bigger than your O. Set a French rolling pin in the center of the fondant and fold one end up over it. Try not to handle the fondant too much. Pick up the pin, then quickly and carefully lay the fondant on the cake. Place a 10-inch square cake board on top and, sandwiching the cake board and the cake drum between both hands, quickly flip the cake over. Remove the cake drum from the top. Use a sharp paring knife to trim the excess fondant away from the outside of the O along the bottom as well as from the middle of the O.

13 Repeat the process to cover and trim the top of the X cake.

14 Center a cake drum on top of each cake and flip the cakes over so the fondant-covered sides are up; remove the cake boards from the top.

15 **Cover the sides of the O cake:** Knead the CMC powder into the remaining gray fondant (about 1½ pounds). For the sides of the O, measure the circumference and the height of the cake. Roll out a band of fondant that is ⅛ inch thick, slightly longer than the circumference, and about 1 inch wider than the cake is tall. Cut this band so that the long ends are perfectly straight and the width is ½ inch wider than the cake is tall. Carefully pick up the band and wrap it around the outside of the cake, making sure the bottom edge is flush with the cake drum. Smooth it with a fondant smoother. Where the fondant ends overlap, cut a clean seam through both layers using a ruler and paring knife, then remove the excess. Do not trim away the ½-inch rise above the cake.

16 For the middle of the O, measure the inner circumference and again roll out a band that is ⅛ inch thick and 1 inch wider than the cake is tall. Cut that band to a width that is ½ inch wider than the cake is tall. Roll up the band onto itself, insert it into the center of the O, and unroll it against the sides of the cake; smooth it onto the cake with a small nonstick rolling pin. To cut the clean seam where the ends overlap, insert the paring knife straight down and cut through both layers.

17 Roll out a small piece of fondant until it is ⅛ inch thick. Use #805 and #809 round piping tips to cut 17 rings, which will become the sockets of the marquee lights.

18 For the sides of the X, roll out a sheet of fondant until it is ⅛ inch thick. Cut several bands that are ½ inch wider than the cake is tall. Working around the X little by little, cut the bands to fit, starting with the little V's at the top and bottom of the X: Set the bottom edge of a fondant piece flush with the cake drum and the inner angle of the V, and use a fondant smoother to smooth the sides. You always want the band to be longer than the surface you are covering, as you can trim away the excess. Continue to cover the remaining sides with fondant bands, smoothing with the fondant smoother and trimming away excess at the sides with a paring knife—but always leaving the ½-inch rise above the cake. When trimming away the excess fondant, make sure you hold the blade of your knife flush against the cake, and use the middle of the blade rather than the tip.

19 Before painting the cake, mark the positions of the lights. For the O, in a clockwise direction, use a toothpick to mark eight equally spaced points where your lights will sit. For the X, mark the center with a toothpick and then mark two evenly spaced points per leg of the X, for a total of nine markings.

21 To accentuate the seams for a welded-metal look, use the paintbrush to dab a thicker coat of luster paint right along the seams.

20 In a small bowl, mix silver and black luster dust with clear food-grade alcohol, adding the alcohol a little at a time until you get a paint-like consistency. With a soft paintbrush, paint the entire surface of each cake, including the top, sides, and borders, making sure you always brush in the same direction to create a weathered-metal look.

22 **Add the marquee lights:** Position the fondant rings over the toothpick marks you made and glue them down with piping gel. Pipe a tiny bit of piping gel into the center of each ring and set a gumball on top. Present these cakes to your loved ones and watch their faces light up!

To: Mr. Cole
Love: Yo

Gift Box

SERVES 10 TO 15

Sometimes appearances can be deceptive. Anyone who's attempted to recreate a Beyoncé video knows that dancing in heels isn't as effortless as she makes it look.

Dancing, like caking, is an art form, and while it's a lot of fun, it often requires hours of patience and practice. So if you're wondering why a "simple" gift box cake is in level 3, understand that learning how to keep a cake square and straight is a lot like learning how to twirl effortlessly in six-inch heels.

This cake will help you perfect your crumb coat and icing skills. It's one of those cakes where what happens on the inside, particularly during the multiple icing phases, affects the look of the outside. For your gift box to look like a real, straight-edged box, the icing can't be crooked, and that takes Bey-level practice. But this cake isn't all "werk." The fun of it is in how versatile it is—each time you make it, you can customize the size, color, and pattern as you hone your skills. Now get your wind machine out and get ready to upgrade your cake game!

Gift Box

3

CAKE IT TO THE LIMIT

⚒ Tools

12-inch square cake pan (3 inches deep)

Sir Squeeze-A-Lot bottle (see page 52)

Nonstick mat or board

Rolling pins: small nonstick and wooden

Ruler and fabric measuring tape

Round piping tips: #803 and #807

Serrated knife

10-inch square cake drum

Spatulas: small offset and large straight

Bench scraper

Fondant smoother

Set square

4 (10-inch) square cake boards

Paintbrush

Paper and tools to create a template

Straight pin

🗏 Ingredients

1½ recipes	Yo's Ultimate Chocolate Cake batter (page 22)
1 recipe	Yo's Italian Meringue Buttercream (page 30)
	Gel food colorings: lemon yellow, pink, royal purple, and turquoise
1 recipe	Yo's Simple Syrup (page 34)
5 ounces	gum paste
	Confectioners' sugar for rolling fondant
3 pounds	white fondant
	Clear piping gel
6 ounces	black fondant
½ recipe	Yo's Royal Icing (page 38)
	Vegetable shortening for kneading gum paste if needed
	Food coloring marker for writing

Day 1: Prep It

1 Preheat the oven to 350°F. Line the bottom of a 12-inch square cake pan with parchment paper (see "How to Bake a Cake" on page 44).

2 Prepare the cake batter according to the recipe. Pour it into the prepared pan. Bake for 1 hour, or until a toothpick inserted in the center comes out clean, rotating the pan halfway through. Transfer to a wire rack and let cool completely in the pan. Cover tightly with plastic wrap and refrigerate overnight.

3 Prepare the buttercream according to the recipe. Put 1 cup of buttercream into each of three separate bowls. Color each bowl of buttercream a different color (see page 58). I made yellow, pink, and purple. Cover the bowls, including the uncolored buttercream, tightly with plastic wrap and refrigerate.

> Since this cake is black and white on the outside, any buttercream colors will look great on the inside, so use your favorites!

4 Prepare the simple syrup according to the recipe. Let cool to room temperature. Pour into your Sir Squeeze-A-Lot bottle and refrigerate.

5 Dye 4 ounces of the gum paste a bright teal by kneading in a little less than ⅛ teaspoon turquoise food coloring. On a nonstick mat or board, using a small nonstick rolling pin, roll out half of the teal gum paste to about 1/16-inch thickness. Wrap the remaining teal gum paste tightly in plastic wrap and set aside in a cool, dry place.

6 **Make the bow pieces:** Using a paring knife and ruler, cut the rolled-out gum paste into two strips, each 1 inch wide and 7 inches long. Fold the strips into loops like ribbon. Glue the tips together with a dab of water and then pinch the ends together. You'll need two loops for the bow on the gift box, but I like to have one or two extra loops on hand in case one breaks, so feel free to make extra. Set aside to dry overnight.

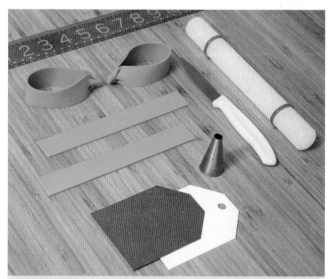

7 **Make the gift tag pieces:** Roll out the remaining white gum paste paper thin (or as thin as possible). Using a template or a gift tag as a guide, cut out a tag shape. Use a #803 piping tip to cut out a hole in the top of the tag. Set aside to dry overnight.

Day 2: Cake It

1 Remove all the buttercreams from the fridge and let them come to room temperature. This may take a few hours.

2 Remove the cake from the pan and peel off the parchment. Set the cake right side up, and level it using a serrated knife and ruler (see page 48).

3 Use the ruler to mark the midpoint along the edge of the cake on all four sides. Using a ruler and serrated knife, use these marks as a guide to divide your cake into 4 equal squares.

4 Lay out the four squares on a clean work surface and shower them with simple syrup. Let the syrup soak in fully before continuing.

5 On a 10-inch square cake drum, stack and fill the cake squares, spreading a different color of buttercream (but not the uncolored one) over each layer with a small offset spatula. (Do not spread buttercream on the top cake layer.)

6 After the cake layers are stacked and filled, measure the height of the cake on all sides to make sure it's even. If it's not perfectly level, use the ruler and serrated knife to even it out.

7 Use the offset spatula to crumb coat the cake with some of the uncolored buttercream (see page 56). Transfer to the fridge to chill for 20 to 30 minutes, until the crumb coat is firm to the touch.

8 Using a large straight spatula, apply another layer of buttercream over the crumb coat, trying to get it as smooth as possible. (Reserve some buttercream for touch-ups later.) Square cakes are hard to ice, so don't be discouraged if it's not perfect. Just take your time building up corners and edges until you're happy. Chilling the cake in between icing attempts really helps! Return the cake to the fridge for 20 to 30 minutes, until the buttercream is firm to the touch.

> A bench scraper can come in handy for smoothing sides and getting corners sharp.

9 Measure the width and height of all four sides of the cake. Dust the work surface with confectioners' sugar and roll out four slabs of white fondant until ¼ inch thick and slightly wider and taller than the sides of the cake. Trim them to the exact height of the sides of the cake.

10 Apply two slabs of the white fondant to two opposite sides of the cake one at a time, smoothing the fondant onto each side with a fondant smoother. Trim away the excess from the sides with a sharp paring knife, holding the blade of the knife flush with the side of the cake as you slowly cut downward. Repeat to cover the other two sides.

11 Knead the white fondant scraps together and roll out into a piece that's ¼ inch thick and slightly larger than the top of the cake. Using a ruler as your guide, cut out a perfectly straight line along one side of the fondant. Using a set square to ensure you have a perfect corner where the two sides meet, cut a second straight line. Do not cut the other two sides; you want them to slightly hang over those sides of the cake.

12 When all four sides are covered with fondant, the fondant may still be higher than the cake in some areas. Fill these with uncolored buttercream in order to level off the top.

13 Pick up the fondant and line up the perfect corner with one corner on top of the cake. Make sure the two cut sides of the fondant slab are flush and lined up with those two sides of your cake.

14 **Trim away the excess fondant from the other two sides:** Place a 10-inch square cake board on top of the cake. Put one hand underneath the cake drum and one hand on top of the cake board; holding the cake firmly but without squeezing it, quickly flip the cake upside down. Remove the cake drum. Cut away the excess fondant on the base, holding the blade of the knife flush against the side of the cake. Leave the cake upside down for now.

15 **Make the sides of the lid:** Roll out another slab of white fondant until ⅛ inch thick and 8 inches square. Cut it into four rectangular bands that are each 1¾ inches wide. In the same manner as you applied the fondant to the sides of the cake, brush the backs of two bands with a bit of piping gel, then smooth the bands onto two opposite sides of the cake at what is now the bottom flush with the cake board. Trim both bands flush with the sides of the cake. Apply bands on the other two sides, trimming away the excess.

16 **Make the border design for the lid:** Roll out a slab of black fondant as thinly as possible. Cut out strips that are longer than your lid and ⅜ inch wide. Working with one side of the lid at a time, start with the bottom and top borders. Brush two strips with piping gel and glue each one to the top and bottom of the lid. Trim away the excess at both ends. Repeat this step on the remaining three sides of the lid. Center the cake drum on top of the cake and flip the cake right side up.

17 Cut two of your ⅜ inch wide black fondant strips into eight pieces just a little taller than the sides of the lid. Using piping gel, apply a strip vertically to each side of each corner, overlapping the horizontal border strips. Cut diagonally through both the long and the short strips where they overlap in each corner to mimic the mitered corners of a picture frame.

18 Complete the border around the top edges of the lid by applying four long black strips, allowing them to overlap in the corners and then trimming them diagonally like a picture frame.

19 If the seams on the corners are very noticeable, you can hide them by patching with a thin layer of royal icing. Because this cake is white, you won't have to worry about color matching!

20 Now it's time to create the polka-dot wrapping paper design. Roll out a sheet of black fondant as thin as you can, then use a #807 piping tip to cut out polka dots.

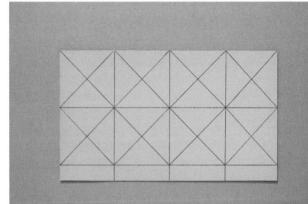

21 For a perfect polka dot pattern, create a grid template. Measure the width and height of one side of the cake (not including the lid). Cut out a piece of paper to that size. Divide the long side of the paper into four equal columns. Take note of the column width measurement and use it to mark the short sides of your paper, starting at the top and working toward the bottom. Draw horizontal lines at these marks to create rows. The bottom row will not be equal. The template should now look like a grid. Draw an X through all of the full size squares.

Believe me, math isn't my favorite subject. If you find achieving the perfect polka-dot pattern overwhelming, skip the template and freehand it, arranging the polka dots however you like. After all, gift wrap comes in lots of different styles!

22 Set the paper template against the side of the cake so that the shortest row is at the bottom. With a straight pin, poke holes through the paper and into the fondant underneath at all the corners of the boxes and the middle of each X. Remove the template. Use piping gel to apply the black dots to the white fondant where the pinpricks are—except down the middle line: don't put polka dots there, as that is where the gum paste ribbon will go. Repeat to decorate the remaining three sides of the cake, trimming the dots at the edges to make them look like they wrap around the corners of the gift box.

23 My favorite part of wrapping a gift is putting a pretty bow on top! Unlike fondant, gum paste sets up pretty quickly, so I suggest rolling out and applying only two bands at a time. If the gum paste starts cracking as you work with it, start over by kneading it (with a little vegetable shortening if needed) and rerolling. Don't be discouraged—if at first you don't succeed, try again! Measure from the base of one side, up and over the lip of the lid, and to the middle of the top of the cake. Roll out some of the teal gum paste as thin as possible into a piece that is that length and a little more than 2 inches wide. Working quickly, cut it into two bands that are 1 inch wide. Use piping gel to attach one band on one side, from the midpoint of the base, up over the lid, and to the center of the top. Repeat on the opposite side, then trim the bands where they meet in the center.

24 Roll out two more bands in the same fashion and apply them to the other two sides. Trim them where they meet in the center, but this time pinch each end in the same way you pinched the bow loops. This will start to create the look of the knot for the bow.

25 **Create the tails of the bow:** Roll out more teal gum paste and cut two bands 1 inch wide and shorter than the side bands. Cut one end of each on the diagonal. Pinch the straight ends, then use piping gel to attach the tails to the top center of the cake where the other gum paste pieces meet. Create movement and slight waves in the tails and glue them down with piping gel.

26 Attach the bow loops to the top with royal icing as glue. Roll out a bit more teal gum paste and cut a band that is the width of the bow loops. Wrap it over where the bow loops join so it looks like the knot in the center of the bow, then remove it and trim it to fit. Attach it to the bow with royal icing.

27 Write a message on the gift tag with a food coloring marker. To make the string to attach it, take a small ball of leftover teal gum paste and roll it out with your fingertips into a thin cord. Feed the cord through the hole in the tag and pinch it together at the ends. Set the tag on your gift and tuck the ends of the string under the bow. No one will be disappointed with this chocolaty gift!

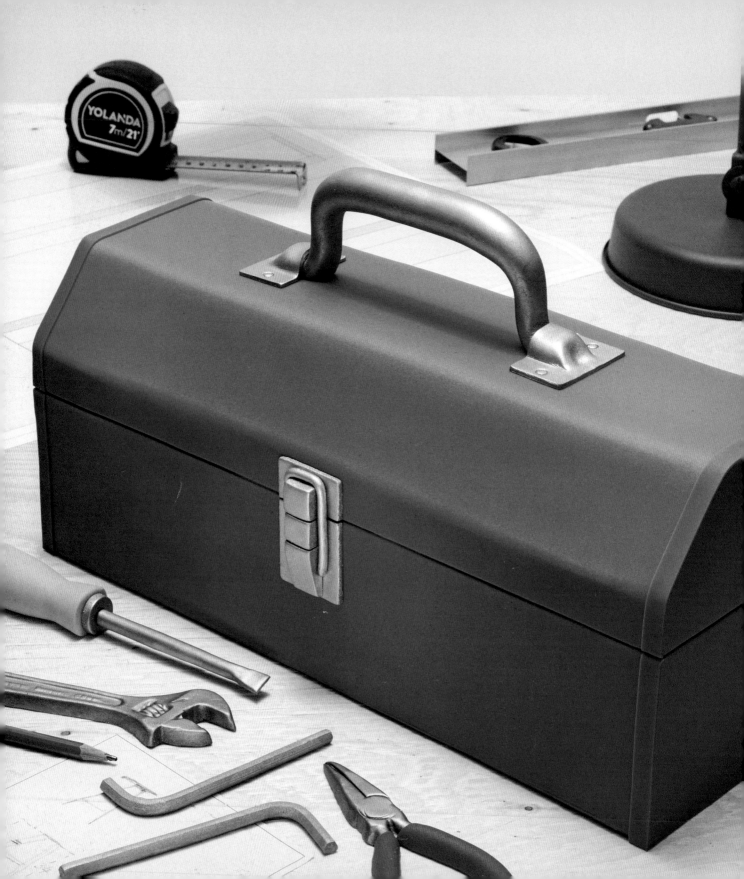

Toolbox

We all have that handy person in our lives who saves the day when something is broken (and thank goodness for them!). This cake is for that person, or for anyone in your life who loves to work with tools and build things. My dad had a passion for woodworking and would make all kinds of things with his tools. He had sooo many tools that even a toolbox this big wouldn't have had room for them all. He'd leave them lying all over the house, too, and I remember following him around, picking them up, and putting them back in his toolbox. I'm such a neat-freak!

This cake *looks* simple but involves lots of opportunities to practice various techniques and to pick up a few new tricks. The body of this cake, with its clean, straight edges, will help you master icing techniques, while creating the front latch provides a good opportunity to practice working on gum paste details. And you'll love making all the tools using molds and paints. Using a chocolate mold for gum paste is a great way to ease into sculpting and creating fine details. If you're ready to start *building up* your cake skills, this cake gives you all the tools you need!

Toolbox

3

CAKE IT TO THE LIMIT

✕ Tools

2 (11 × 15-inch) cake pans (3 inches deep)

Sir Squeeze-A-Lot bottle (see page 52)

Nonstick mat or board

Rolling pins: small nonstick, wooden, and French

Clay extruder with small round and hexagon faceplates

Tool chocolate mold

Veining and bone sculpting tools

6-inch lollipop stick

Round piping tips: #8 and #809

Paintbrushes

Serrated knife

Ruler and fabric measuring tape

18-inch square cake drum, trimmed to 15 × 18 inches

Spatulas: small and large offset; large straight

Fondant smoother

Foam core board

🥤 Ingredients

3 recipes	Yo's Coconut Cake batter (page 28)
1 recipe	Yo's Chocolate Swiss Meringue Buttercream (page 32)
1 recipe	Yo's Italian Meringue Buttercream (page 30)
2 recipes	Yo's Simple Syrup (page 34)
1 pound	gum paste
1 ounce	black fondant
	Golden yellow gel food coloring
	Vegetable shortening
	Clear piping gel
	Confectioners' sugar for rolling fondant
3½ pounds	blue fondant
	Luster dust: silver and matte black
1 ounce	red fondant
	A few pieces of raw spaghetti

Day 1: Prep It

1 Preheat the oven to 350°F. Line the bottoms of two 11 × 15-inch cake pans with parchment paper (see "How to Bake a Cake" on page 44).

2 Prepare the cake batter according to the recipe. Scrape the batter into the prepared pans, dividing it evenly, and spread so that it is smooth in the pan. Bake for 1 hour 10 minutes, or until a toothpick inserted in the center comes out clean, rotating the pans halfway through. Transfer to wire racks and let cool completely in the pans. Cover tightly with plastic wrap and refrigerate overnight.

3 Prepare the two buttercreams according to the recipes. Cover both bowls tightly with plastic wrap and refrigerate.

4 Prepare the simple syrup according to the recipe. Let cool to room temperature. Pour into your Sir Squeeze-A-Lot bottle and refrigerate.

5 **Color the gum paste for the tools and details:** Mix 12 ounces of the gum paste with the black fondant. Knead together to create a nice gray color for most of the tools as well as the toolbox handle and hardware. To color gum paste for the handle of the screwdriver, mix the remaining 4 ounces gum paste with golden yellow food coloring, kneading it to even out the color. Have fun with this and choose any shade you'd like.

I often color gum paste with fondant rather than food coloring as it's easier to knead in and prevents staining of my hands and work surface.

6 **Create the handle for the top of the toolbox:** If the gum paste starts drying as you work with it, knead it (with a little vegetable shortening if needed) and start over. On a nonstick mat or board, using a small nonstick rolling pin, roll out 3 ounces of gray gum paste into a cord that is about ⅝ inch thick and thinner at the ends. Bend it downward at two points, then bend the ends out in the opposite direction. Trim the ends slightly with a sharp paring knife, leaving a ¾-inch base. Set the handle aside, lying flat, to dry overnight.

7 For the hinges, roll some of the gray gum paste into a cord about ¼ inch thick; cut this into three 2¼-inch lengths. Use a paring knife to lightly score each piece horizontally all around in three places to make the indents on the hinges; don't cut all the way through. Set aside to dry.

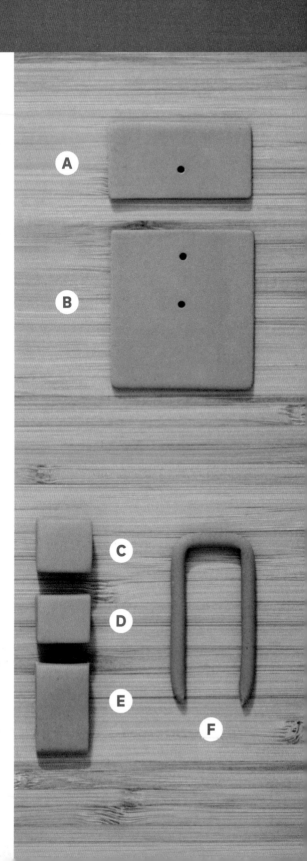

8 For the front clasp, you'll make six pieces. Roll out gray gum paste ¹⁄₁₆ inch thick to a 1¼ × 2½-inch rectangle. Cut it into two pieces: one 1 × 1¼-inch piece (A), which will be the base plate affixed to the lid, and one 1½ × 1¼-inch piece (B), which will be the base plate affixed to the toolbox body.

9 Roll out a piece of gray gum paste ½ inch thick; cut a strip from it that is ⅝ inch wide and 2½ inches long. From that strip, cut two ⅝-inch squares (C and D), leaving you with one longer rectangle—these will be the three top clasp pieces. Taper one end of the longer rectangle (E) by rolling the end thinner with the rolling pin and then using a paring knife to trim the rectangle to the same width as the two squares.

10 For the latch that loops over the top of the clasp (F), roll some of the gray gum paste into a cord. Push the cord through a clay extruder fitted with a small round faceplate. Curve the extruded cord around the three top clasp pieces and trim the ends so it looks like it enters the bottom rectangle at the midpoint. Let dry slightly for about 30 minutes so it holds its shape. Carefully pull the latch loop off and set it and all the clasp pieces aside for a couple of hours to firm up.

11 Cut ½ inch off a toothpick on one end and gently push the piece of toothpick halfway into the back of the thick gum paste pieces (C, D, E) to create a hole in each. Use these marks to help line up where the pilot holes on the base plates (A and B) will go: Starting with the top square (C), insert the piece of toothpick into the hole you've created, pointy end out. Then center and line up the bottom of C with the bottom of the smaller baseplate piece (A). Press down gently to leave a mark with the toothpick. Center and line up the top of the square (C) with the top of the larger baseplate piece (B). Press down gently to leave another mark here with the toothpick.

12 Transfer the toothpick into the thicker rectangle piece (E). First lay C on top of B, with both tops lined up using C as a guide for where E will go. Use the toothpick to make a mark in B. Set all the clasp pieces aside separately to dry.

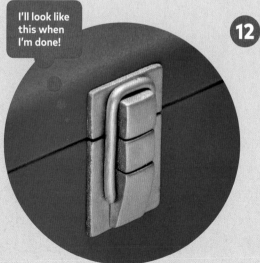

I'll look like this when I'm done!

Toolbox

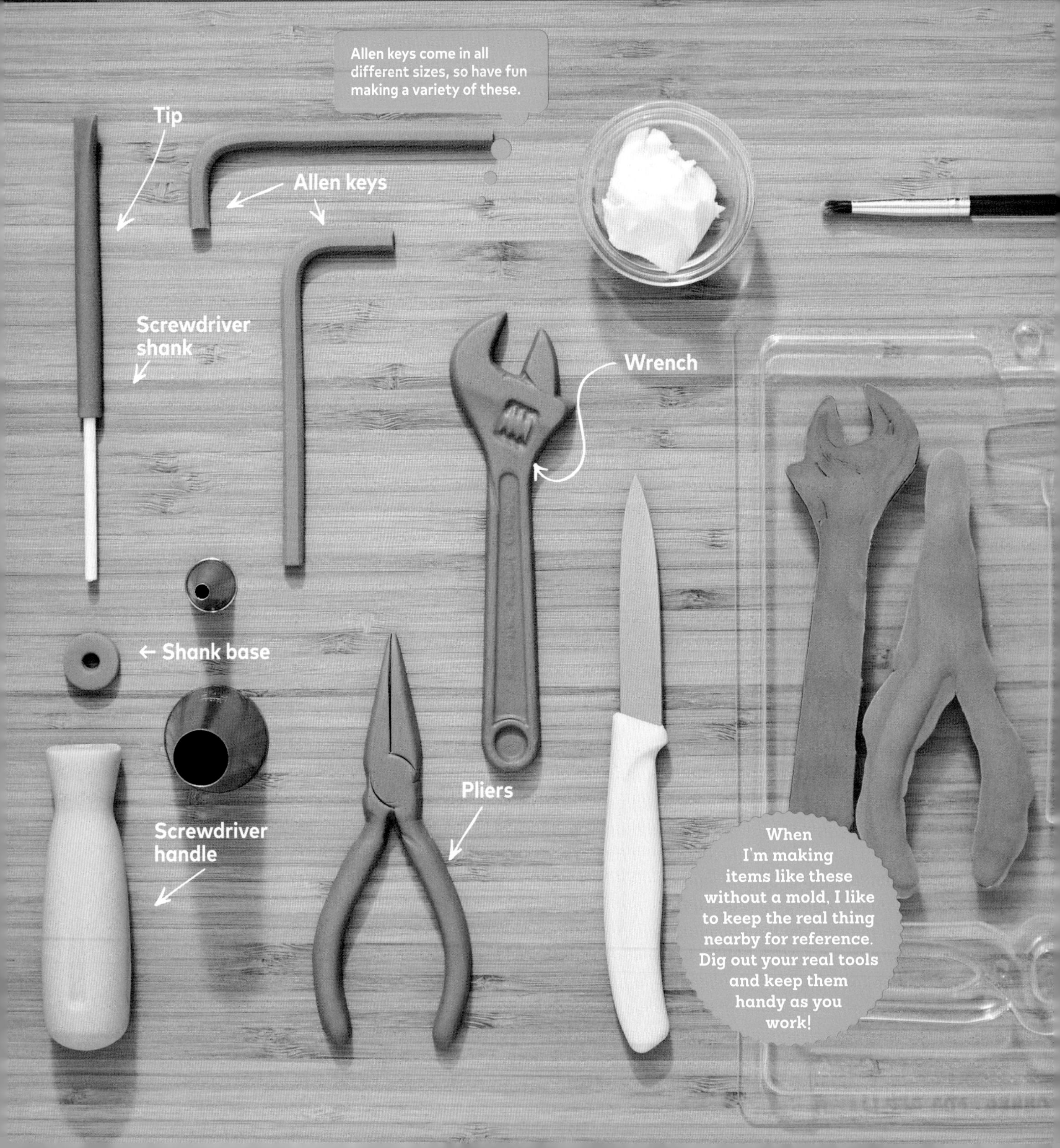
Allen keys come in all different sizes, so have fun making a variety of these.
Tip
Allen keys
Screwdriver shank
Wrench
Shank base
Pliers
Screwdriver handle
When I'm making items like these without a mold, I like to keep the real thing nearby for reference. Dig out your real tools and keep them handy as you work!

13 **Create the tools:** Prepare a chocolate mold by brushing a thin layer of vegetable shortening into the tool shapes you'll be making. Roll a piece of gray gum paste into a cord that is about the size of the first tool you're making. Gently press it into the mold with your fingertips to fill in the shape. Don't worry if you've put a little too much gum paste in the mold—you'll have a chance to trim the excess later. Repeat to make the remaining tools. Flip the mold over and check to see if there are any air pockets; if there are, press the gum paste some more, and add more gum paste to the molds if needed. Once you're happy with how the mold is filled, set it aside for 10 minutes for the gum paste to set.

14 Rub a bit of shortening on the blade of a paring knife, and cut any excess gum paste away so that the gum paste in the mold is flush with the top surface of the mold. Take a moment to tidy up where you cut: Put some shortening on your fingertips and smooth out the surface if it appears rough. Let the gum paste set in the mold for an additional 30 minutes, then turn the mold over and gently tap the tools out onto a clean work surface. Neaten up the edges again with a sharp knife, then set the tools aside to dry.

15 **Make the Allen (hex) keys:** Soften about 2 ounces of the gray gum paste by kneading in a little shortening. Roll some of the gum paste into a cord, then push it through the clay extruder fitted with a hexagon faceplate. Trim two nice sharp ends and bend it at a right angle near one end. Set aside to dry.

16 **Create the screwdriver handle:** Roll the yellow gum paste into a thick cord, making one end of it round and slightly thicker. Cut it to the desired handle length (about 4 inches long). About 1 inch down from the cut end, pinch the cord in while rolling it on the work surface, to create an indent. Use a veining sculpting tool to create indents on all four sides of the screwdriver, to mimic a real handle's grip feature. With a 6-inch lollipop stick, poke a hole in the cut end of the handle, going halfway down the handle. Remove the lollipop stick.

17 **Make the screwdriver shank base:** Roll out a bit of gray gum paste about ¼ inch thick. Use a #809 piping tip to cut out a circle, then cut a smaller circle from the middle with a #8 piping tip to make a washer shape.

18 **Make the screwdriver shank:** Brush piping gel onto the lollipop stick. Roll out a thin band of gray gum paste over 4 inches long and wrap it around the stick, leaving a short piece extending past the end (this will become the tip). Cut a clean seam down the length, removing the excess gum paste, then roll the stick on the work surface to smooth the gum paste. With your fingers, flatten the piece of gum paste sticking out from the end, then cut it to look like a flat-head screwdriver. Trim excess gum paste from the opposite end, leaving 2 inches of the lollipop stick exposed (this will be inserted back into the handle). Set all the pieces aside to dry.

19 You will have a little gray gum paste left over. Wrap it tightly in plastic wrap and set aside in a cool, dry place.

Day 2: Cake It

1 Remove the two buttercreams from the fridge and let them come to room temperature. This may take a few hours.

2 Remove the cakes from the pans and peel off the parchment. Set the cakes right side up, and level them using a serrated knife and ruler (see page 48). Flip the cakes over and remove the caramelization from the bottoms using the same technique. Using the serrated knife, cut each cake in half lengthwise so you have four 5½ × 15-inch pieces.

3 Lay out the four cake pieces on a clean work surface and shower them with simple syrup. Let the syrup soak in fully before continuing.

4 On the trimmed cake drum, stack and fill the cake layers, spreading a dollop of chocolate buttercream over each layer with a large offset spatula (see page 54). (Do not spread buttercream on the top cake layer.) Transfer to the fridge to chill for 20 to 30 minutes, until the buttercream is firm to the touch.

5 **Start shaping the toolbox:** Along the top of the cake, mark a shallow line about 1 inch in from each long edge lengthwise. On both long sides, measuring up from the base, make a mark at the 4¾-inch point. (If you like, make a paper template to help guide you as you cut.) Use the serrated knife to cut at a 45-degree angle from the line on the top down to the line on the side. Cut from one end in to the halfway point of the cake, then turn the cake around and cut from the other end. Repeat on the other long side of the cake.

6 Use a straight spatula to crumb coat the cake with Italian meringue buttercream (see page 56). Transfer to the fridge to chill for 20 to 30 minutes, until the crumb coat is firm to the touch.

7 Apply another layer of Italian meringue buttercream over the crumb coat, trying to get it as smooth as possible. Return it to the fridge for 20 to 30 minutes, until the buttercream is firm to the touch.

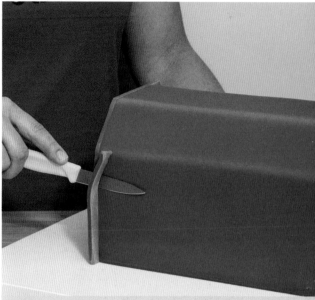

8 Measure the length of the cake, and then measure from the base of one long side, up and over the top, to the base of the other side. Dust the work surface with confectioners' sugar and, using a wooden rolling pin, roll out the blue fondant into a rectangle ⅛ inch thick and slightly larger than those measurements. Set a French rolling pin in the center of the fondant and fold one end up over it. Try not to handle the fondant too much—use the rolling pin to move it instead of your hands. Pick up the pin, then quickly and carefully drape the fondant over the cake from front to back. Smooth it using a fondant smoother, making sure to accentuate the angled sides. Trim the excess fondant away from the base and sides using a paring knife held flush against the side of the cake.

9 **Cover the ends of the cake with blue fondant:** Measure the height and width of each end of the cake. Knead together the fondant scraps and roll out into two panels that are ⅛ inch thick and slightly larger than those measurements. Cut a perfect straight edge along one side of each panel that will be along the base of the toolbox. Line one panel up against one side of the cake with the straight edge flush with the cake drum and use the fondant smoother to smooth it onto the cake. Use the paring knife to trim away the excess fondant from the top and sides. Repeat on the other side.

10 Make the tools and toolbox hardware look more realistic: First brush a thin layer of shortening over all the tools and hardware (except the handles of the pliers and screwdrivers). Brush silver luster onto the surface of the tools and hardware to coat them completely. You can play around with the tones of your metals and darken them by adding some matte black dust, as I did with the wrench, pliers, and Allen keys.

> I do this on a paper towel, one color at a time, so I can easily collect and reuse the luster dust.

11 Create a red grip for the handles of the pliers: Divide the red fondant in half and roll out each half as thin as you can. With the pliers lying flat, brush each handle with piping gel, drape a piece of the fondant over each handle, and smooth it with your hands. You don't have to cover the underside. Trim away the excess.

12 To finish the screwdriver, use piping gel to attach the gum paste washer to the flat end of the handle, then insert the screwdriver shaft.

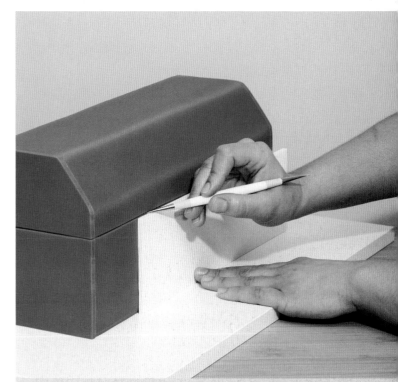

13 Cut a foam core board to 3½ inches high and hold it against any side of the cake. Using a bone sculpting tool, and using the top of the board as a guide, make an indent all around the cake to look like the line where the lid and the rest of the toolbox meet.

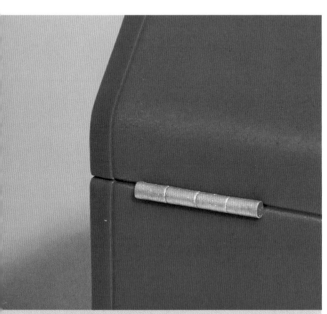

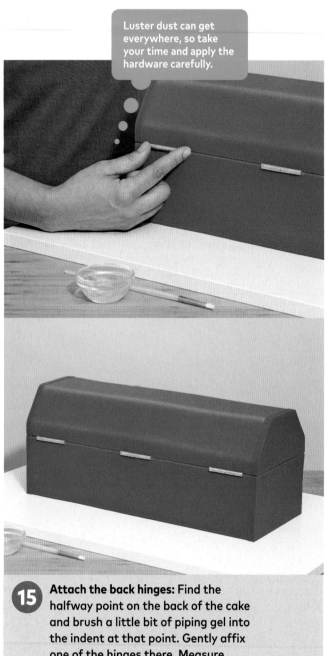

Luster dust can get everywhere, so take your time and apply the hardware carefully.

14 **Add the finishing details:** Start with the side seams. Knead the fondant trimmings together and roll out into two thin bands long enough to go from the base at the front of the cake, up and over the top, to the base at the back. Cut these into two ¼-inch-wide strips and apply over the seams of the side panels using piping gel. Once the bands are attached, use the foamcore board and the veining tool to press into the existing indent underneath.

15 **Attach the back hinges:** Find the halfway point on the back of the cake and brush a little bit of piping gel into the indent at that point. Gently affix one of the hinges there. Measure 1 inch in from one side and affix a second hinge there. Repeat on the other side with the third hinge.

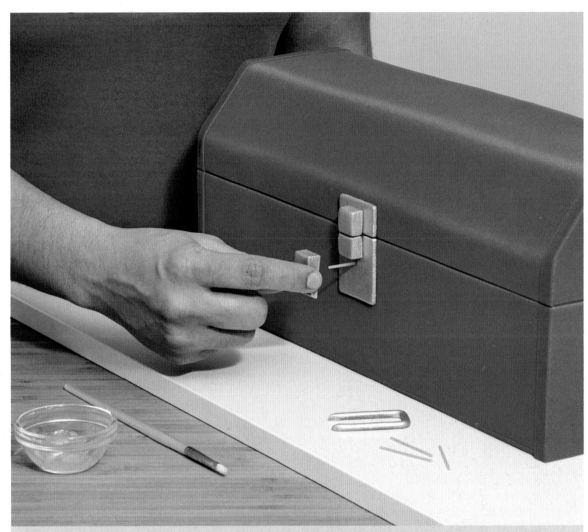

16 **Add the clasp to the front of the cake:** Use piping gel to glue the two base plate pieces in the middle of your toolbox, above and below the indented line. Insert short pieces of spaghetti through the three pilot holes and about 2 inches into the cake. Brush piping gel onto the thicker square and rectangle top clasp pieces and gently push them onto the spaghetti until they meet the base plates. Make sure that the spaghetti doesn't come all the way through.

See that toolbox? I made it! And you can, too!

17 **Add the latch to the clasp:** Apply piping gel to the back of the gum paste loop and very carefully attach the loop around the clasp.

18 The final touch is the toolbox handle. You'll need to make two more gum paste pieces that will serve as "handle brackets." Roll out the leftover gray gum paste as thin as possible and cut out two 1¼ × 1½-inch rectangles. Brush the pieces with shortening, then with silver luster (the same as you did with the other hardware). Smooth the gum paste pieces over each end of the handle to look like brackets that would hold the handle down. If you need to, use a paring knife to trim the edges of the gum paste to keep the rectangles sharp and square.

19 When you're happy with the shape of the brackets, use the #8 round piping tip to make impressions into both sides of each bracket to look like rivets. Working quickly and leaving everything intact, carefully pull the brackets off the handle. Using piping gel, glue the handle to the center of the toolbox lid. Apply piping gel to the underside of the brackets and glue them into place over each end of the handle. Now get to work ... eating cake!

Soft Serve Cone

SERVES 10 TO 12

My favorite thing to do when I'm not caking is make ice cream—or eat it! I'm completely obsessed with ice cream, and even wanted to start an ice cream channel on YouTube, but *How To Ice Cream It* just didn't have the same ring to it, you know? There's something about ice cream that makes me feel like a kid again—especially when it's a delicious soft serve cone, which brings back memories of chasing the ice cream truck.

Ice cream paired with cake makes for the perfect celebration. That's why my first YouTube birthday cake was an Ice Cream Cone in my favorite flavor, mint chocolate chip. And when Camp Cake—a fun live-stream bake-along where I cake with YoYos from around the world—fell close to my birthday, my YoYos and I made Ice Cream Sundae Cupcakes together to celebrate. So I *had* to make sure an ice cream cake made it into this book. This time around, I'm caking a classic, Instagram-worthy summertime soft serve. The challenge with this cake is in the coloring of the cone. I often find it can be tricky getting subtle, natural colors just right, but it's great practice and the payoff is so worth it. You're gonna melt over this one. #yum

Soft Serve Cone

CAKE IT TO THE LIMIT

⚔ Tools

1 (6-inch) round cake pan (3 inches deep)

3 (5-inch) round cake pans (3 inches deep)

3 (4-inch) round cake pans (3 inches deep)

Kitchen scales

Sir Squeeze-A-Lot bottle (see page 52)

Serrated knives (large and small)

Ruler and fabric measuring tape

Cake boards: 2 (10-inch) round, 1 (8-inch) round, 4 (6-inch) round, 2 (3-inch) round, and 1 (4-inch) round

Spatulas: small offset and large straight

Circle cutters: 1½-inch, 3-inch, and 4-inch

Rolling pins: wooden and French

Fondant smoother

Strip cutters: #2 and #3

Paintbrush

Protractor (optional)

Masking tape

12-inch round cake drum

4 (¼-inch-wide × 12-inch-long) wooden cake dowels

Garden shears (to cut dowels)

🥤 Ingredients

½ recipe	Yo's Ultimate Chocolate Cake batter (page 22)
1 recipe	Yo's Ultimate Vanilla Cake batter (page 24)
1 recipe	Yo's Italian Meringue Buttercream (page 30)
1 recipe	Yo's Simple Syrup (page 34)
3 pounds	white fondant
	Gel food colorings: ivory and buttercup yellow
	Confectioners' sugar for rolling fondant
	Clear piping gel
½ recipe	Yo's Royal Icing (page 38)
	Clear food-grade alcohol
1 pound	chocolate fondant

Day 1: Prep It

1 Preheat the oven to 350°F. Line the bottoms of one 6-inch, three 5-inch, and three 4-inch round cake pans with parchment paper (see "How to Bake a Cake" on page 44).

2 Prepare the cake batters according to the recipes. Pour the batters into the prepared pans, dividing them among the pans as follows:

For the chocolate batter:

2 (4-inch) round pans:
½ pound batter each

1 (5-inch) round pan:
1 pound batter

For the vanilla batter:

1 (4-inch) round pan:
½ pound batter

2 (5-inch) round pans:
1 pound batter each

1 (6-inch) round pan:
1 pound batter

   Spread the batter so that it is smooth in the pans. Bake the 4-inch cakes for 35 minutes, the 5-inch cakes for 40 minutes, and the 6-inch cake for 45 minutes, or until a toothpick inserted in the center comes out clean, rotating the pans halfway through. Transfer to wire racks and let cool completely in the pans. Cover tightly with plastic wrap and refrigerate overnight.

3 Prepare the buttercream according to the recipe. Cover the bowl tightly with plastic wrap and refrigerate.

4 Prepare the simple syrup according to the recipe. Let cool to room temperature. Pour into your Sir Squeeze-A-Lot bottle and refrigerate.

5 Color 2 pounds of the white fondant to look like an ice cream cone, using ivory and buttercup yellow food coloring (see page 62). Start by coloring a couple of ounces of white fondant, and if it gets too dark, knead in more white fondant. When you're happy with the color, wrap the fondant tightly in plastic wrap and set aside in a cool, dry place.

Subtle colors, like the cone color, can be tricky to get right, so have a live model nearby, and lots of patience: work slowly and add the color to the white fondant in small increments.

Day 2: Cake It

1 Remove the buttercream from the fridge and let it come to room temperature. This may take a few hours.

2 Remove the cakes from the pans and peel off the parchment. Set the cakes right side up, and level them using a serrated knife and ruler (see page 48). Flip the vanilla cakes over and remove the caramelization from the bottom using the same technique. (You don't need to remove caramelization from the chocolate cakes.) Make sure all the vanilla cakes are the same height and all the chocolate cakes are the same height. Stack the humps of your chocolate cakes on top of each other and press them gently so they stick together. These will become the tip of the ice cream.

3 Lay out all the cakes on a clean work surface (treating the pressed-together came humps as one cake) and shower them with simple syrup. Let the syrup soak in fully before continuing.

4 Your cone will have two parts, the "cup" and the "lip." Start by building the cup: On a 10-inch round cake board, stack and fill the vanilla cakes, with the two 5-inch cakes on the bottom and the 4-inch cake on top, spreading buttercream over each layer with a small offset spatula. (Do not spread buttercream on the top cake layer.) Transfer to the fridge to chill for 20 to 30 minutes, until the buttercream is firm to the touch.

5 Now make the lip of the cone: Put the 6-inch vanilla cake on a 10-inch round cake board and, using a 4-inch circle cutter, mark a 4-inch circle on the top of your cake. Using your serrated knife, carve a rounded edge from the 4-inch circle down to the outer edge of the base of the cake. When finished, the top of the cake should have a 4-inch diameter and the base a 6-inch diameter.

If you'd like, hold a 3-inch round cake board on top of the cake to make it easier to carve.

6 Retrieve the cup of the cone from the fridge. On the top center of the stack of cake, mark a 3-inch circle with a circle cutter. With a serrated knife, carve in an A-line cut to the outside edge of the base of the cake, carving all around; the top of the cake should have a 3-inch diameter and the base should have a 5-inch diameter. Set aside the two cone pieces.

7 Make the "ice cream" from the three chocolate cakes: Using a 3-inch circle cutter, cut one of the 4-inch round cakes down to 3 inches in diameter. Now you'll have 3-inch, 4-inch, and 5-inch round cakes. Using a small serrated knife, round the top and bottom edges of each of the three cakes all the way around so each looks like a rounded patty. Cut an extremely slight angle off the top of each cake so that they will lean slightly when stacked. Perfect the rounded top edges if needed. Place each cake on a 6-inch round cake board.

8 Make the top peak of the ice cream swirl: Using a 1½-inch circle cutter, cut a circle from the center of the stacked-together chocolate cake humps. Using the small serrated knife, carve the circle into a tiny peak like the top of a soft-serve ice cream. Place the top peak on a 6-inch round cake board.

Cake It to the Limit **241**

9   Crumb coat all the cakes—the four ice cream pieces, the cup of the cone, and the lip of the cone—with some of the buttercream using straight and offset spatulas (see page 56). Transfer them to the fridge to chill for 20 to 30 minutes, until the crumb coat is firm to the touch.

10   **Add the cake boards to the cone:** Place a 3-inch round cake board on top of the cup of the cone, then apply another layer of buttercream over the sides, trying to get it as smooth as possible. Place a 4-inch round cake board on top of the cone lip and apply buttercream over the sides.

11   Ice all of the ice cream pieces. Reserve a bit of buttercream to use in step 14. Return all the cakes to the fridge to chill for 20 to 30 minutes, until the buttercream is firm to the touch.

12   **Cover the cup of the cone:** Measure the height of the base of the cone and its circumference at the base (the 5-inch-diameter end). Dust a work surface with confectioners' sugar and, using a wooden rolling pin, roll out a piece of the cone-colored fondant that is ⅛ inch thick and large enough to surround the cup. To pick up the fondant, set the French rolling pin on one end of the fondant and roll the pin with the fondant around it (like wrapping paper onto a roll) until all the fondant is wrapped around the pin. Try not to handle the fondant too much—use the rolling pin to move it instead of your hands. Pick up the pin with the fondant wrapped around it, then quickly and carefully unroll it around the side of the cup, smoothing it out with a fondant smoother. Where the ends of the fondant overlap, line up a ruler along the seam and use a sharp paring knife to cut through the overlapping fondant. Remove the excess from on top and underneath to create a clean seam. Trim away any excess at the top and the base of the cup.

13   **Cover the lip of the cone:** Measure the cake from the base of one side, up and over to the base of the other side. Roll out a piece of cone-colored fondant that is ⅛ inch thick and slightly larger than that size. Drape the fondant over the cake (leaving the board on) and smooth it out with a fondant smoother and your hands.

14   **Cover the other side of the lip:** Place an 8-inch cake board on top of the cone lip. Put one hand underneath the bottom cake board and one hand on top of the top cake board; holding the cake firmly but without squeezing it, quickly flip the cake over. Remove the top cake board to reveal the flat side. Crumb coat the flat side with the reserved buttercream. Roll out a circle of cone-colored fondant that is ⅛ inch thick and slightly larger than the flat side. Place it on the flat side and trim any excess with the paring knife.

15   **Add the cone details to the cup:** For the vertical strips, roll out some of the remaining cone-colored fondant. Use a #2 strip cutter to cut out strips to create the cone's grid pattern. You'll add 12 vertical strips to the cone. Think of your cone as a clock. Start by adding one strip vertically, brushing it with a bit of water so it adheres, and call this 12 o'clock. Using a fabric measuring tape, find 6 o'clock and glue a vertical strip there. Measure and identify 3 o'clock, add a strip there, and do the same at 9 o'clock. Add two strips between each of those positions, making sure they're equally spaced. When all the vertical strips have been added, trim them to 4½ inches high.

17 Add the cone details to the rim of the cone: Make 8 strips of cone-colored fondant using a #3 strip cutter. Make them about 5 inches long, then cut them in half. To position the strips on the top of the cone, I used a protractor to help me measure out and place the strips evenly around the lip. If you don't have a protractor, use the clock method again: glue on strips at the 12, 3, 6, and 9 o'clock positions, from the outer edge toward the center. Then attach three additional strips, equally spaced, between each of those positions.

18 Use a 4-inch circle cutter centered in the middle to trim all the strips to an equal length.

16 Add the horizontal strips: Make a small mark between all the vertical strips at 1¼ inches and 2¾ inches up from the base. This is where you'll place the horizontal strips. If you need more strips at this point, roll out more of the cone-colored fondant and cut with the strip cutter. Trim those strips to fit the spaces between the vertical strips, tapering the ends to adjust to the curve, and attach them where you made the marks. At 4½ inches from the base, where all the vertical strips end, attach two strips, laid end to end, to create a horizontal strip all the way around.

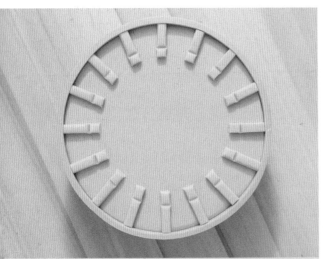

19 **Finish the trim:** Measure the circumference of the lip. Roll out a band of fondant that is ⅛ inch thick and as long as that circumference; cut it to ½ inch wide. Using piping gel, attach the band to the lip of the cone, wrapping the band around the top of the lip and making sure it lines up with the top of the 16 strips to create a rim much like on a real cone.

20 **Flip the cup of the cone right side up:** Place a loop of masking tape in the center of the 3-inch cake board currently on the top of the cup. Center a 12-inch round cake drum on top of the tape, with the cake drum's covered side down. Put one hand underneath the bottom cake board and one hand on top of the cake drum; holding the cake firmly but without squeezing it, quickly flip the cake over so that the narrow, tapered end of the cone is now at the bottom. Remove the 10-inch cake board from what is now the top of the cup.

21 **Assemble the cone:** You'll be inserting dowels into the cup of the cone to support the weight of the lip of the cone and the ice cream. Place a 1½-inch circle cutter in the center of the top of the cup and use one of the dowels to make six marks around the outside edge of the circle cutter. Trim the dowels to the height of the cake. Insert a dowel straight down and all the way into the cake at one of the marks, and use a pencil to mark a cut line level with where the dowel emerges from the surface of the cake. Remove the dowel and use that mark to cut six dowel pieces to the right height from three dowels. (Reserve the fourth dowel for later.) Insert your dowels straight down into the cake at the marks you made, making sure the top ends are flush with the top of the cake.

22 **Add the lip of the cone:** Spread some royal icing on the top of the cup of the cone, over the dowels, but not spreading too close to the edge. Center the lip of the cone on top of the cup, making sure that both fondant seams—on the cup and on the edge of the lip—are on the same side.

23 **Conceal the seam where the cup and lip meet:** Measure the circumference of the lip where it meets the base of the cone, and roll out a band of cone-colored fondant that is ⅛ inch thick and the length of the circumference; trim it to ¼ inch wide. Use piping gel to attach it to the cone, wrapping it around the seam.

24 As a final touch to the cone, to give the color a little more depth, give the entire cone a light coat of paint. Mix ivory food coloring with enough clear food-grade alcohol to make a thin paint consistency. Use a paintbrush to brush over the entire surface of the cone. Pay special attention to the corners of the grid pattern, brushing away the paint that will naturally pool there.

25 **Make the vanilla ice cream:** To create the soft-serve twist, you'll need to cover the ice cream cake layers in two parts: vanilla and chocolate. Starting with some of the white fondant, roll out a circle that is ⅛ inch thick and with a diameter that is 2 inches larger than the cake layer you're covering. Using a cake pan or other circular template the same size as your circle of fondant, cut part of a circle out of the fondant to make a crescent moon shape. (For example, to cover the 5-inch cake layer, roll out a 7-inch circle of fondant and then use a 7-inch pan or template to cut out part of the circle.)

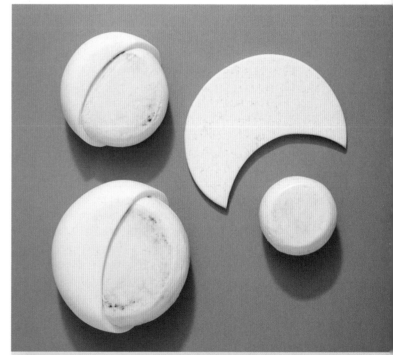

26 Drape the moon-shaped fondant over the cake layer so that it covers half of the cake layer. Carefully smooth the fondant and tuck it underneath the cake. Trim away the excess with a paring knife. Repeat to cover the other two cake layers (but not the top peak).

27   **Make the chocolate ice cream:** For each cake layer, roll out a circle of chocolate fondant that is ⅛ inch thick and 2 inches larger in diameter than the cake layer you're covering. Cut each in half to create a half-circle of fondant that will comfortably fit into the gap left by the white fondant. Drape the fondant over the cake, making sure the round edge of the chocolate is snug against the crescent moon of the white fondant. Carefully smooth the chocolate fondant into the vanilla and tuck it underneath the cake, trimming away the excess. Repeat to cover the other two cake layers (but not the top peak).

28   **Cover the top peak:** Use the same technique you used to cover the ice cream cake layers but in reverse, so that the crescent moon shape is cut out of the chocolate fondant and the white fondant is a half circle. (I just wanted more chocolate at the top!) Use your fingertips to gently shape the fondant into a peak.

29   **Assemble the cone and ice cream:** Spread royal icing into the center of the top of the cone. Place a 3-inch cake board on top. Spread another bit of royal icing on top of the cake board and add the 5-inch ice cream layer. Spread a little bit of royal icing on top of that and add the 4-inch layer, lining up the vanilla-chocolate twist. Spread royal icing on top of that and add the 3-inch layer, again lining up the twist.

30   Sharpen one end of the last dowel and insert it all the way through the middle of the cake right down to the bottom. You may need a hammer to get it through all the boards and the drum. The dowel should now be hidden in the top 3-inch cake layer. Spread a little royal icing on the top of the 3-inch layer and set the top peak on top. Now you're ready to serve up this giant soft serve!

Toy Bulldozer

SERVES 14 TO 16

My son just loves construction sites. From real-life digs to toys, if there's a bulldozer on the scene, he's all smiles. And having been to quite a few toddler parties over the last couple of years, I can assure you he's not alone. Turns out most preschoolers tend to share his obsession, making this the perfect cake to serve to pint-sized partygoers. My son is four now, and not surprisingly, this replica of a toy bulldozer is his favorite cake in the whole book (though he still hasn't forgiven me for cutting into it). Each toy bulldozer tends to have slightly different detailing, so if you're making this cake for a little one in your life, I suggest making it extra special by customizing it to perfectly match their own toy.

Along the way, you'll get to practice doweling, carving, and creating fondant and gum paste details. Exercise your creativity by propping it before serving. I used chocolate pebbles and candy bricks to set the scene, with cotton candy smoke as a sweet added touch. I guarantee you, there isn't a kid around who won't dig this!

Toy Bulldozer

3

CAKE IT TO THE LIMIT

Tools

12 × 18-inch cake pan

Sir Squeeze-A-Lot bottle (see page 52)

Nonstick mat or board

Rolling pins: small nonstick, wooden, and French

Serrated knife

Ruler

Small offset spatula

Cake boards: 4 × 8 inches for the base, 3¼ × 4½ inches for the cab

16-inch cake drum to hold the finished cake

3 (¼-inch) wooden cake dowels

Garden shears (to cut dowels)

Clay extruder with round and flat faceplates

Paintbrush

Strip cutters: #1 and #2

Circle cutters: 1-inch and 2½-inch

Round piping tips: #807 and #809

Ingredients

2 recipes	Yo's Ultimate Chocolate Cake batter (page 22)
1 recipe	Yo's Italian Meringue Buttercream (page 30)
	Gel food colorings: lemon yellow and golden yellow
1 recipe	Yo's Simple Syrup (page 34)
8 ounces	gum paste
	Confectioners' sugar for rolling fondant
3½ pounds	yellow fondant
1 pound	white fondant
2 pounds	black fondant
½ recipe	Yo's Royal Icing (page 000)
	Vegetable shortening
	Clear piping gel
1 ounce	red fondant

Props and styling (optional)

1 cup	chocolate cookie crumbs for "dirt"
	Chocolate pebbles
	Block-shaped candies to look like bricks at a construction site
	White cotton candy for the "smoke" coming out of the exhaust pipe

Day 1: Prep It

1 Preheat the oven to 350°F. Line the bottom of a 12 × 18-inch cake pan with parchment paper (see "How to Bake a Cake" on page 44).

2 Prepare the cake batter according to the recipe. Pour the batter into the prepared pan. Bake for 50 minutes, or until a toothpick inserted in the center comes out clean, rotating the pan halfway through. Transfer to a wire rack and let cool completely in the pan. Cover tightly with plastic wrap and refrigerate overnight.

3 Prepare the buttercream according to the recipe. Color 4 cups by stirring in 1 tablespoon lemon yellow and ¼ teaspoon golden yellow food coloring. Cover the bowl tightly with plastic wrap and refrigerate. (Cover and refrigerate or freeze the remaining buttercream for another use.)

4 Prepare the simple syrup according to the recipe and let cool to room temperature. Pour into your Sir Squeeze-A-Lot bottle and refrigerate.

> The further in advance you can make the blade, the better, as gum paste details get stronger and last longer with more time to set.

5 To make the bulldozer's blade, dye the gum paste with ¼ teaspoon lemon yellow and ⅛ teaspoon golden yellow food coloring. On a nonstick mat or board, using a nonstick rolling pin, roll out the gum paste until ⅛ inch thick. Trim the gum paste into a 5 × 9-inch rectangle. (Your bulldozer cake will be approximately 9½ inches wide, and you'll want the blade to be a similar width.) Fold the gum paste over the length of a greased rolling pin (or other curved surface) and set aside to dry. Tightly wrap the remaining gum paste in plastic wrap and set aside.

Day 2: Cake It

1 Remove the yellow buttercream from the fridge and let it come to room temperature. This may take a few hours.

2 Remove the cake from the pan and peel off the parchment. Set the cake right side up, and level it using a serrated knife and ruler so that it's 1½ inches in height (see page 48). Set aside the hump, because you will use it later.

4 Shower all the cake pieces with simple syrup to keep the cake moist and delicious. Let the syrup soak in fully before continuing.

3 **Using the ruler and serrated knife, trim the cake into eight pieces:**

- First, cut a 2½-inch-wide strip lengthwise from the cake, then cut that in half crosswise, creating two 2½ × 9-inch strips (A); set the two strips aside. These will become the two tracks that will sit on each side of the truck.

- This leaves you with a 9½ × 18-inch slab. Cut it into three rectangles as follows: two 5½ × 9½-inch (B) rectangles and one 7 × 9½-inch (C) rectangle. The two 5½ × 9½-inch rectangles, along with the trimmed hump, will become the body of the bulldozer.

- Cut the 7 × 9½-inch rectangle into four smaller rectangles, each 3½ × 4¾ inches (D). These will be used to create the cab and the hood.

- Cut a 5½ × 9½-inch rectangle from the center of your cake hump (E). Using the serrated knife and ruler, level it to 1 inch in height.

5 **Make the bulldozer body:** Using a small offset spatula, fill and stack the three 5½ × 9½-inch layers with yellow buttercream, centering the stack on the 4 × 8-inch cake board.

6 **Make the cab:** Fill and stack three of the four smaller (3½ × 4¾-inch) rectangles with yellow buttercream, centering the stack on the 3¼ × 4½-inch cake board. Transfer the body and the cab to the fridge to chill for 20 to 30 minutes, until buttercream is firm to the touch.

7 **Make the hood:** Level the remaining small rectangle to 1 inch in height. This will be placed on the top of the body.

8 Take the two 2½ × 9-inch strips (the tracks) and round off all four corners with a serrated knife.

Cab

Hood

Body

Tracks

9 Retrieve the largest stack of cake (the body) from the fridge and carve the shape of the bulldozer body with a serrated knife, rounding off the corners and indenting the sides at the top of the cake, for two-thirds of the length of the cake (see photo in step 16 for clarity). Taper the bottom edges to meet the edge of the cake board.

10 Take the smaller stack (the cab) out of the fridge and round off the top, then trim the sides and front so the cab slopes slightly toward the bottom. Then, cutting on the diagonal, trim off the front corners. Make sure to trim off the front corners of the cake board that may still be sticking out.

11 Set the hood piece on top of the body so you can visualize the bulldozer shape; with the serrated knife, round the top edges of the hood. Remove the hood piece and set it aside.

12 Use the small offset spatula and the yellow buttercream to crumb coat (see page 56) all the cake stacks and pieces separately, including the track pieces (lay them down flat on their wide sides). Transfer all the cake pieces to the fridge to chill for 20 to 30 minutes, until the crumb coat is firm to the touch.

13 Apply another layer of buttercream over the crumb coat, trying to get it as smooth as possible. Return to the fridge to chill for 20 to 30 minutes, until the buttercream is firm to the touch.

14 **Apply yellow fondant to the body, tracks, and hood pieces:** Measure the bulldozer body. Dust the work surface with confectioners' sugar and roll out a sheet of yellow fondant that's ⅛ inch thick and large enough to cover it in one piece. Set a French rolling pin in the center of the fondant and fold one end up over it. Try not to handle the fondant too much. Pick up the pin, then quickly and carefully drape the fondant over the body of the bulldozer and smooth it with your hands. Trim away the excess with a sharp paring knife. Roll out two smaller pieces of yellow fondant and drape them over the tracks; smooth the fondant and trim away the excess. Roll out a piece of yellow fondant and cover the hood; smooth the fondant and trim away excess.

15 **Make gray fondant and apply it to the cab:** Knead together the white fondant and 1 ounce of the black fondant to make gray. Roll out the gray fondant and cover the cab; smooth the top and all four sides and trim away excess at the corners. Roll out the black fondant and cover the gray fondant, starting with two smaller pieces on the sides and then draping one longer piece over the front, top, and back. Trim the bottom edges.

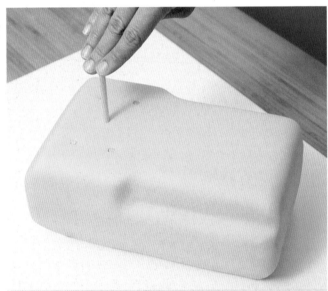

16 Put the bulldozer body piece on the 16-inch cake drum. Insert a dowel into the body of the cake where the cab will sit, and mark a cut line level with where it emerges from the surface of the cake. Remove the dowel and use that mark to cut five dowel pieces from three dowels. Insert the dowels all the way into the body of the cake where the cab will sit, with one in the center of the area and the other four about an inch in from each corner. The dowels should not extend above the fondant.

17 Place the cab on top of the bulldozer body, keeping the cake board underneath the cab; use a little royal icing to adhere it.

18 **Place the hood onto the body of the bulldozer:** First, measure the space between the cab and the front of the bulldozer to make sure the hood will fit now that it's covered in fondant and bigger than before. You may need to trim the end of the hood that will be nestled against the cab, using a sharp paring knife. Place the hood on top of the bulldozer body, using a little royal icing to adhere it.

19 **Create the windows in the cab:** Using a sharp paring knife, cut away rectangles in the black fondant on each side of the cab to reveal the gray fondant underneath. Leave a ½-inch border of black around each window to frame it.

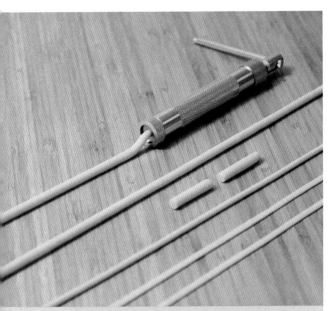

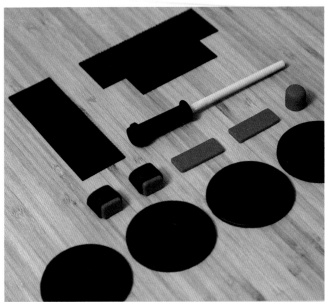

20 **Create some basic details using fondant and a clay extruder:** Mix some of the leftover yellow fondant with a little shortening to soften it, then roll the fondant into several cords. Push each cord through the clay extruder using the round and flat faceplates to make borders to go around the hood and around the cab. These add nice details and help to cover up seams. Attach the details to the fondant by brushing a little piping gel on them.

21 Cut four black fondant bands 1¼ inches wide and as long as the four sides of the bulldozer's base. Use a little piping gel to attach the bands to the base of the bulldozer, and trim the seams with a paring knife. This will give the bulldozer the appearance of being raised from the ground.

22 **Make the grilles for the back and front of the bulldozer:** Roll out some of the black fondant, then use a strip cutter to lightly score the fondant to make grille markings. Cut out two pieces that will fit the front and back of the bulldozer (an upside-down T shape for the front and a rectangle the width of the back). Brush piping gel onto the black fondant pieces and attach them to the bulldozer.

23 Have fun adding other details like lights, lighting mounts, and an exhaust pipe using black and red fondant and simple tools such as a paring knife and a ruler. I made two small lighting mounts (black with red inside) for the top of the cab, one larger red light for the top of the cab, two red front lights, two back lights, and an exhaust pipe (black fondant wrapped around a dowel; trim the fondant off one end of the dowel and stick it into the cake).

24 Create the tracks: Roll out and cut two bands of black fondant that are each long enough to go around the outside of each track. Roll out and cut a similar band to make the treads for the tracks. Use a strip cutter to cut narrow strips of black fondant, cut them to the width of the band, then attach them with piping gel, leaving ½ inch of space between them to create the treads.

25 Create the four wheels: Roll out black fondant and cut four circles with the 1-inch circle cutter and four with the 2½-inch circle cutter (for eight circles total). On the smaller circles, use the #807 and #809 round piping tips to indent concentric circles. With piping gel, attach the smaller circles to the larger circles. Add fondant spokes to the wheels using a strip cutter and paring knife to make eight spokes per wheel, attaching them with piping gel. Add the bands between the two wheels on each side, cutting out a curve with the 2½-inch circle cutter at each end of the bands to fit them to the wheels.

I took my son's bulldozer when he wasn't looking—don't tell!

27 **Add the bulldozer blade:** Very carefully lift the dried and set gum paste from the rolling pin. Using royal icing, attach the blade to the front of the bulldozer.

28 Add edible props around the bulldozer— cookie crumb dirt, chocolate pebbles, and candy bricks. At the last minute (because cotton candy dissolves quickly), stick a puff of cotton candy on the end of the exhaust pipe to look like smoke to complete the look. Now get ready to *dig* in!

26 **Create the arms of the bulldozer blade:** Mix together equal parts yellow gum paste and yellow fondant. (This mixture, called "50/50," is stronger than fondant and not as quick to dry out as gum paste.) Roll it out until ¼ inch thick, then cut two ¼-inch-wide strips that are long enough to extend from the back of the hood down over the front of the bulldozer to the cake board in front. Attach the strips to each side of the bulldozer body with piping gel. The ends in front will be hidden by the blade.

Crown

SERVES 20 TO 24

When I first started *How To Cake It* on YouTube, some fans referred to me as the Queen of Cakes, and what can I say, the name stuck. I mean, who am I to refuse that title? But this Crown cake isn't just a nod to my nickname—I actually caked it for you, my YoYos, who are all queens and kings to me, as well as for my son, who is the prince of my world. I actually made a smaller blue version for him a few years ago, so this cake holds a lot of sentimental value.

Like all queens, this cake is majestic. But don't put my crown on a pedestal—have fun putting your own spin on it. Once you've got the carving and structure set, you can customize it any way you like. This crown always looks great in lots of colors, so try experimenting with your favorites. Be creative with designing different shaped jewels, laying out the jewels in varying patterns and playing with the ornamentation. I've made a few variations of this cake, and they've all looked completely different. So if you're looking to cause a royal stir, this cake is the perfect fit for any feast!

Crown

3

**CAKE IT
TO THE
LIMIT**

🍴 Tools

4 (9-inch) round cake pans (3 inches deep)

Sir Squeeze-A-Lot bottle (see page 52)

Silicone gem molds: teardrop, rectangle, round, and square-cut jewel shapes

Rolling pins: wooden and French

Circle cutters: 4-inch and 1½-inch plain, and 1¾-inch scalloped

4 (¼-inch) wooden cake dowels, one of them sharpened at one end

2½-inch circle of foamcore

Paintbrushes	2 (6-inch-diameter, 1-inch-thick) Styrofoam disks glued together to make a 2-inch-thick disk
6-inch lollipop stick	
Serrated knives	
Ruler and fabric measuring tape	14-inch round cake drum
Spatulas: small and large offset	Masking tape
Cake boards: 2 (14-inch) round, 1 (6-inch) round, and 1 (8-inch) round (optional)	Straight pin
	Lace-pattern embossing tool (such as FMM textured lace set #1)
	1¾ × 2-inch heart cookie cutter

🥤 Ingredients

For the cake

3 recipes	Yo's Ultimate Chocolate Cake batter (page 22)
1½ recipes	Yo's Italian Meringue Buttercream (page 30)
	Pink gel food coloring
2 recipes	Yo's Simple Syrup (page 34)
	Confectioners' sugar for rolling fondant
½ recipe	Yo's Royal Icing (page 38)
4 pounds	pink fondant
2 (2.5 gram) jars	pink luster dust
	Clear food-grade alcohol
3 (4 gram) jars	gold luster dust
1	giant gumball

For the gems and ornamentation

	Gel food colorings: pink, turquoise, and golden yellow
12 ounces	gum paste
1 ounce	black fondant
¼ teaspoon	CMC powder
	Vegetable shortening
6 ounces	white fondant
	Clear piping gel
	Edible spray glaze
3 (2.5 gram) jars	Luster dust: pearl, pink, and teal
	White candy beads or pearls

Day 1: Prep It

1 Preheat the oven to 350°F. Line the bottoms of four 9-inch round cake pans with parchment paper (see "How to Bake a Cake" on page 44).

2 Prepare the cake batter according to the recipe. Pour the batter into the prepared pans. Bake for 1 hour 15 minutes, or until a toothpick inserted in the center comes out clean, rotating the pans halfway through. Transfer to wire racks and let cool completely in the pans. Cover tightly with plastic wrap and refrigerate overnight.

3 Prepare the buttercream according to the recipe. Put 3 cups of the buttercream in a separate bowl and set aside. Color the remaining buttercream by stirring in ½ teaspoon pink food coloring. Cover both bowls tightly with plastic wrap and refrigerate.

4 Prepare the simple syrup according to the recipe. Let cool to room temperature. Pour into your Sir Squeeze-A-Lot bottle and refrigerate.

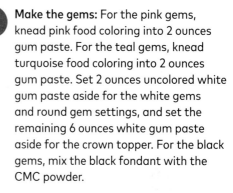

Make these well in advance, as the longer gum paste dries, the better the shape holds.

5 **Make the gems:** For the pink gems, knead pink food coloring into 2 ounces gum paste. For the teal gems, knead turquoise food coloring into 2 ounces gum paste. Set 2 ounces uncolored white gum paste aside for the white gems and round gem settings, and set the remaining 6 ounces white gum paste aside for the crown topper. For the black gems, mix the black fondant with the CMC powder.

6 **Mold the gems:** Rub a little bit of shortening into a silicone gem mold (this will help when releasing the gum paste). Take small pieces of pink, teal, and white gum paste and press them into the desired gem shapes in the mold; let them stand for a few minutes, then remove them from the mold by bending it gently. Make 24 each of the pink, teal, and white gems, plus a few extras in case of breakage. Make about eight white round gem settings and eight black gems. Set aside in a cool, dry place to dry.

Don't dig gems out! Bend the mold gently to keep their shape.

7 Real crowns usually have some sort of ornamentation on the top. For this crown topper, I used a mixture called "50/50" to create a mini cake on a cake stand. To make the 50/50, knead the white fondant with the remaining 6 ounces gum paste, then knead in ¾ teaspoon golden yellow food coloring. Dust the work surface with confectioners' sugar and, using a wooden rolling pin, roll out the yellow 50/50 until ¼ inch thick. Use a 1½-inch circle cutter to cut out three rounds. Using your fingertips, mold a little cherry and stem for the top of the cake.

It'll look like this when it's done!

8 **Make the mini cake stand:** Using a sharpened dowel, poke a hole through the center of a 2½-inch circle of foamcore. Brush piping gel on one side of the foamcore and cover that side with 50/50. Flip it over and trim away the excess. Brush the surface and sides with piping gel, and cover it with 50/50, smoothing around the edges to completely cover the foamcore. Cut away the excess with a sharp paring knife. Puncture both sides of the 50/50 with a lollipop stick where the hole is (so the hole goes all the way through the disk).

9 For the cake stand pedestal, roll out a cord of 50/50 and use your fingertips to shape it freehand to look like the pedestal of a cake stand. Gently push the lollipop stick through the pedestal, then perfect the shape of the pedestal around the stick. Gently remove the stick, leaving the hole. Set all the mini cake and cake stand pieces aside in a cool, dry place to dry. Tightly wrap the remaining 50/50 in plastic wrap and set aside at room temperature.

Day 2: Cake It

1 Remove both buttercreams from the fridge and let them come to room temperature. This may take a few hours.

2 Remove the cakes from the pans and peel off the parchment. Set the cakes right side up, and level them using a serrated knife and ruler (see page 48). Using the serrated knife and ruler, cut the cakes into layers to make a total of eight layers.

3 Lay out all the cakes except for one layer on a clean work surface and give them all a light shower of simple syrup. Let the syrup soak in fully before continuing. Enjoy the extra layer as a snack.

4 **Stack and fill seven of the cake layers:** Using a large offset spatula, spread a dollop of buttercream over each layer, alternating pink and uncolored buttercream. Put a 6-inch round cake board between the third and fourth layers for extra stability. (Do not spread buttercream on the top cake layer.)

5 **Add support:** You'll also need to insert six dowels (three unsharpened dowels cut in half) in a 5-inch circle formation into the top of your cake, flush with the height of it (see page 244, step 21). Transfer the cake to the fridge to chill for 20 to 30 minutes, until the buttercream is firm to the touch.

6 **Shape the cake:** Start by carving what will be the base of the crown when the cake is flipped over. Center the glued-together Styrofoam disks on top of the cake; these will later serve as the crown's base. With the serrated knife, cut from the edge of the disk downward in an A-line motion to about one-third of the way down the cake to create a taper effect. Set aside the Styrofoam disks and place a 14-inch round cake board on top of the cake. Put one hand underneath the bottom cake board and one hand on top of the top cake board; holding the cake firmly but without squeezing it, quickly flip the cake right side up. Remove the cake board from the top.

7 **Make the dip at the top of the crown:** Using a 4-inch round circle cutter, create a light mark at the very top of the crown. Find the center of this circle and use the tip of a paring knife to carve out an indentation that's deepest at the center of the circle.

8 To shape the top half of the crown, use the serrated knife to round off the top as if you were making a giant apple.

9 When you're happy with your crown shape, use a small offset spatula to crumb coat the cake with some of the pink buttercream. Transfer the cake to the fridge to chill for 20 to 30 minutes, until the crumb coat is firm to the touch.

10 Put a loop of masking tape on the center of a 14-inch round cake drum and attach the Styrofoam disks to it, centering them. Spread royal icing onto the top of the Styrofoam. Carefully pick your cake up off its board and set it on top of the Styrofoam disks. Because you used these disks as a guide when you carved, the cake should fit on top perfectly.

11 **Insert the sharpened dowel for stability:** Measure the height of the cake, then subtract the depth of the indentation in the top. Cut the dowel on the unsharpened end to that length. Insert the dowel all the way down through the middle of the cake, piercing through the cake boards in the center of the layers and down into the Styrofoam base. The top of the dowel should be level with or shorter than the bottom of the indentation.

12 Apply another layer of buttercream over the crumb coat, trying to get it as smooth as possible. Return it to the fridge for 20 to 30 minutes, until the buttercream is firm to the touch.

13 **Cover your cake:** Measure the cake from one side of the base (above the Styrofoam), across the top, and down to the other side of the base. (Note: You'll be covering the Styrofoam base with a separate piece of fondant, so this piece only needs to drape over the cake itself.) Dust the work surface with confectioners' sugar and roll out the pink fondant into a circle that is ⅛ inch thick and large enough to cover your cake. Set a French rolling pin in the center of the fondant and fold one end up over it. Try not to handle the fondant too much. Pick up the pin, then quickly and carefully drape the fondant over the crown. Smooth it over the curves of the crown dome with your hands. Some air will get trapped in the top; release it by pricking the fondant with a straight pin and easing the air out. Where the Styrofoam base and cake meet, trim away excess fondant with a paring knife.

15 Dilute the pink luster dust with clear food-grade alcohol, adding the alcohol a little at a time until you get a paint-like consistency. Brush the paint onto the cake, brushing up and down all over the fondant to give it a soft pink sheen. Allow the paint to dry completely (this could take over an hour).

16 **Make the ornamentation:** Roll out some of the leftover yellow 50/50, and from it cut a band the same size as the pink one you made for the base in step 14. Brush the back with a little water and lay it on top of the pink band, trimming where the ends meet.

17 **Create the bands that will run up the sides of the crown:** Measure from the top of the Styrofoam base to the middle of the indentation in the top. Cut eight strips of yellow 50/50 that are that length and ¾ inch wide. Think of the crown as a clock. Start by adding one strip vertically, first brushing the back of the strip with a bit of water so it adheres, and call this 12 o'clock. Attach a second vertical strip opposite that, at 6 o'clock. Cut both strips where they meet so that they're not overlapping. Add two more strips, at 3 o'clock and 9 o'clock. Cut both strips where they meet the 12 and 6 o'clock strips so that they're not overlapping. Attach the remaining four strips between those positions, making sure they're equally spaced and cutting them so they are not overlapping the other strips.

14 Measure the circumference and height of the Styrofoam base. Roll out a strip of pink fondant until ⅛ inch thick, then trim it so it is long enough to wrap around the base and wide enough to cover the height of the base. Brush piping gel onto the Styrofoam. Wrap the strip around the base, gently pressing it onto the Styrofoam. Trim the excess where the ends meet.

18 **Create the "lace" decoration:** Roll out a square of yellow 50/50 until ⅛ inch thick. Use a lace-pattern embossing tool to make decorative embellishments that will add texture and detailing to the crown.

19 Using piping gel, affix the embellishments just above the Styrofoam base to the pink fondant between the vertical yellow bands. Trim along the side of the bands with the paring knife so the lace does not overlap the bands.

20 Roll out some more yellow 50/50, and using a 1¾ × 2-inch heart cookie cutter, cut out eight hearts. Using piping gel, affix them at the base of each of the yellow bands so that they cover the seams where the lace embellishments meet the bands.

If your luster paint is too runny, wait a little while for the alcohol to evaporate. If it thickens too much while you paint, add a little more alcohol as you work.

21 Dilute the gold luster dust with food-grade alcohol, adding the alcohol a little at a time until you get a paint-like consistency that is not too runny. Paint all the yellow parts of the crown gold. Paint from top to bottom and always in the same direction on each element. You may want to use different brush sizes to get into all the nooks and crannies of the details and to carefully paint the edges of the bands. For the best coverage, paint two coats of gold, making sure the first coat is completely dry before starting on the second.

22 **Finish the mini cake topper:** With a toothpick, poke a hole all the way through the giant gumball, then widen the hole with the lollipop stick. To make the "filling" for the mini cake, roll out 50/50 nice and thin, then cut out three scalloped circles using the scalloped cutter. These circles should be a little larger than the 50/50 mini cake layers you made. Glue each one to the top of a mini cake layer using piping gel, then, where the scalloped edge drapes down, smooth it along the side so it looks like the filling of a cake. Mark the center of each of the layers and use the lollipop stick to pierce a hole all the way through each layer.

I do this on a paper towel, one color at a time, as it helps to collect the luster dust so I can reuse it.

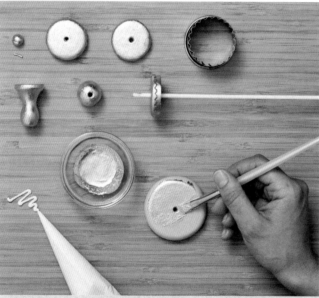

24 **Paint the gems:** Spray the black gems with two coats of edible glaze, letting the first coat dry before applying the second. For the rest of the gems, rub or brush on a very thin layer of shortening, and then brush on the appropriate luster dust. Set aside to dry.

23 **Paint all the topper pieces with gold paint:** your three cake layers, the tiny cherry and stem, the cake stand, and the pedestal. Paint the gumball by swirling it around in a small bowl of gold paint to coat it completely. Set all the pieces aside to dry for at least 1 hour.

26 Add extra details, using candy beads to fill in spaces. The candy beads come in handy for hiding the seams above the styrofoam base.

27 The final touch is assembling the mini cake and cake stand and attaching it to the top of the crown. Insert the lollipop stick into the center of the cake so that most of it is still exposed above the cake, being careful to avoid the dowel in the cake.

28 Add a little dab of royal icing to the indentation at the top of the cake right where the lollipop stick is. Carefully pierce the gumball with a toothpick to prepare it to slide onto the lollipop stick, then use the stick to slightly widen the hole. Slide the gumball down the lollipop stick so it rests in the crown's indentation. Dab some royal icing on top of the gumball. Slide the pedestal of the cake stand down the lollipop stick to rest on top of the gumball. Dab some royal icing on top of that, then slide the top of the cake stand onto the pedestal. Dab some royal icing on top of the cake stand, then slide each cake layer down the lollipop stick, again gluing them together with royal icing. Finally, use royal icing to attach the tiny cherry and stem on top of the mini cake—a fun touch that will make your guests feel like royalty!

25 Get creative applying the gems to the cake! To ensure that the design is even, I use a fabric measuring tape and a straight pin to mark out a pattern before applying the gems. I started with the base and the surface of the hearts. Pipe a tiny bit of royal icing onto the back of the gems and stick them in place. Wipe your fingertips clean before handling gems of different colors, as luster dust easily transfers. I made two different patterns on my bands, alternating as I went around.

Lucky Cat

SERVES 12 TO 16

Japan has always intrigued me, and after Mr. Cake and I visited a few years ago, I've become even more obsessed. We always enjoy our travels, but our trip to Japan was one of our all-time favorites. We haven't been able to get over it and can't wait to return one day.

While we were in Japan, we saw lucky cats everywhere, usually near the doorways of shops and restaurants. Lucky cats are essentially lucky charms, thought to bring good fortune to the owners of the establishments where they reside. To me, they also look like cute little greeters waving hello and goodbye. I thought having a Lucky Cat cake as my final cake would not only give me a way to express my love for Japan but would also be the perfect way to wish you goodbye and good luck in all your caking adventures. It's the most challenging cake in the book, involving lots of sculpting and assembling. But if you've made it this far, and practiced your carving and doweling skills with the other cakes in this level, I think you should try your luck with this one!

Lucky Cat

3

CAKE IT TO THE LIMIT

🔧 Tools

2 (5-inch) round cake pans (3 inches deep)

2 (6-inch) round cake pans (3 inches deep)

Sir Squeeze-A-Lot bottle (see page 52)

Serrated knives (large and small)

Ruler and fabric measuring tape

Cake boards: 2 (10-inch) round, 1 (8-inch) round, 2 (6-inch) round, and 1 (3-inch) round

Spatulas: small offset and straight

3 (¼-inch) wooden cake dowels, one sharpened at both ends

Circle cutter set	Paintbrushes
14-inch round cake drum	Nonstick mat or board
Heatproof mixing bowl	Oval cutters: 2-inch and 3-inch
Veining and pointed sculpting tools (cel stick)	Small teardrop or leaf cutter
1 bendable straw	Round piping tips: #8, #807, #2, and #12
4 (6-inch) lollipop sticks	
Rolling pins: wooden, French, and small nonstick	#2 strip cutter
	Clay extruder with the smallest and largest round faceplates
Fondant smoother	
	5-petal rose cutter
Garden shears (to cut dowels)	Small triangle cutter (optional)

🧃 Ingredients

1½ recipes	Yo's Ultimate Vanilla Cake batter (page 24)
1 recipe	Yo's Italian Meringue Buttercream (page 30)
	Gel food colorings: pink, royal purple, orange, turquoise, golden yellow, and avocado
1 recipe	Yo's Simple Syrup (page 34)
4 pounds	white fondant
4 ounces	gum paste
3 cups	puffed rice cereal
2 tablespoons	unsalted butter
8 ounces	mini marshmallows (half a 16-ounce bag)
½ teaspoon	pure vanilla extract
	Vegetable shortening
	Confectioners' sugar for rolling fondant
½ recipe	Yo's Royal Icing (page 38)
	Clear piping gel
2 ounces	black fondant
	Gold luster dust
	Clear food-grade alcohol
	A piece of raw spaghetti

Day 1: Prep It

1 Preheat the oven to 350°F. Line the bottoms of two 5-inch and two 6-inch round cake pans with parchment paper (see "How to Bake a Cake" on page 44).

2 Prepare the cake batter according to the recipe. Scrape the batter into the prepared pans, filling them halfway, and spread so that it is smooth in the pans. Bake the 5-inch cakes for 50 minutes and the 6-inch cakes for 60 minutes, or until a toothpick inserted in the center comes out clean, rotating the pans halfway through. Transfer to wire racks and let cool completely in the pans. Cover tightly with plastic wrap and refrigerate overnight.

3 Prepare the buttercream according to the recipe. Put 1 cup of buttercream into each of three separate bowls. Color one with pink food coloring, one with royal purple, and one with orange. Cover the bowls, including the uncolored buttercream, tightly with plastic wrap and refrigerate.

4 Prepare the simple syrup according to the recipe. Let cool to room temperature. Pour into your Sir Squeeze-A-Lot bottle and refrigerate.

5 **Color 6 ounces of the white fondant:** Dye 2 ounces teal, 2 ounces light purple, and 2 ounces pink by kneading in turquoise, royal purple, and pink food coloring (see page 62). Wrap each ball individually with plastic wrap and set aside in a cool, dry place. Wrap the remaining uncolored fondant and set aside as well.

6 **Color the gum paste:** Dye 2½ ounces yellow, 1 ounce purple, and ½ ounce green by kneading in golden yellow, royal purple, and avocado food coloring. Wrap each ball individually with plastic wrap and set aside in a cool, dry place.

> I found this cake to be the most challenging in the book, but also the most rewarding. Make sure you set aside two full days—or even three. It involves a lot of time-consuming freehand work. Believe me, this one will take some patience, but the payoff is sweet!

I wish you luck making this cake!

Day 2: Cake It

1 Remove all the buttercreams from the fridge and let them come to room temperature. This may take a few hours.

2 Remove the cakes from their pans and peel off the parchment. Set the cakes right side up, and level them using a serrated knife and ruler (see page 44). Flip the cakes over and remove the caramelization from the bottoms using the same technique. Using the serrated knife and ruler, cut the cakes in layers to make a total of eight layers.

3 Lay out all the cakes on a clean work surface and shower them with simple syrup. Let the syrup soak in fully before continuing.

4 **Build two cakes, one 6-inch and one 5-inch:** On a 10-inch round cake board, stack and fill the 6-inch cake layers, using about half of each of the colored buttercreams and spreading a different color over each layer with a small offset spatula. For the 5-inch cake, first poke a pilot hole through the center of a 3-inch round cake board using a sharpened dowel. Tape the 3-inch board to a 10-inch round cake board. Stack and fill the 5-inch cake layers centered over the 3-inch board, alternating the buttercream colors in the same order. Chill both cakes for 20 to 30 minutes, until the buttercream is firm to the touch.

5 **Carve the body:** The 6-inch cake will be used for the cat's body. Center a 3-inch circle cutter on top of the cake to use as a guide. With the serrated knife, carve down from the edge of the cutter to make a barrel shape, tapering the cake in at the bottom as much as at the top. Transfer the body to a 14-inch cake drum.

The good thing about puffed rice cereal is it can be easily sculpted, cut, and reworked as needed.

6 **Carve the head:** The 5-inch cake will be used for the cat's head. Use the same technique as you did for the body, but use a 2¾-inch circle cutter as a guide and carve the cake into more of a sphere, tapering the bottom down to about 3 inches to meet the 3-inch cake board. Set the head on top of the body to see how they fit together, and make any necessary adjustments. Separate the head from the body and place it back on the 3-inch board.

7 Use offset and straight spatulas to crumb coat each cake with the uncolored buttercream. Chill for 20 to 30 minutes, until the crumb coat is firm to the touch (see page 56).

8 **Make the puffed rice parts:** Put the rice cereal in a heatproof bowl. Melt the butter in a small saucepan over medium heat. Add the marshmallows to the melted butter and stir with a wooden spoon, letting the marshmallows melt slowly. When the marshmallows are nearly melted with just a few lumps remaining, remove the pot from the heat and quickly stir in the vanilla. Pour the hot marshmallow mixture over the rice cereal and stir until well combined.

9 **Make the legs:** You want the legs to look as if the cat is sitting upright on its haunches. Grease your hands with shortening to prevent sticking. Pull out a handful of the cereal mixture and compress and sculpt it into two legs, making sure to shape both a thigh and a foot on each. Sculpt both legs at the same time so you get them as symmetrical as possible. Use a cel stick to create the line dividing the thighs from the feet. Attach the legs by pressing them to the cake body.

10 **Make the right arm:** Pack and sculpt the cereal mixture into an arm that will curve onto the cat's belly. You can also roll the mixture to get the desired shape. When you're happy with the arm, attach it by pressing it to the cake body; make sure the hand rests close to the thigh and the top of the arm sits a little below the neck. (If it's too high up it will interfere with adding the collar later.)

🐱 Lucky Cat

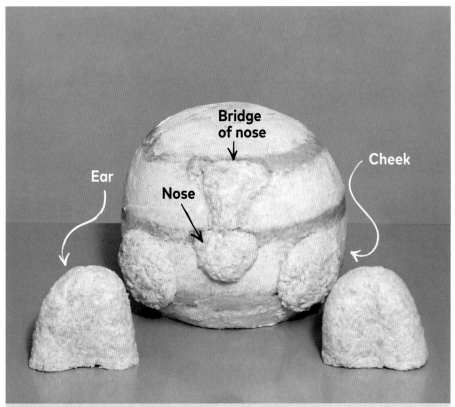

Bridge
of nose

Cheek

Ear

Nose

15 **Make the left arm:** Trim the top of a bendable straw about 1¾ inches from the bend; trim the long end about 3¼ inches from the bend. Cut one lollipop stick to 3 inches and one to 4 inches. Insert the 3-inch stick into the shorter part of the straw and the 4-inch stick into the longer part. This should leave you with an L shape.

11 **Make the facial features:** You'll want to create two cheeks, and a forehead extending into a bridge and nose. For the cheeks, create two patties with a small amount of the cereal mixture, then perfect the edges by cutting with a 2-inch circle cutter. Attach them to the face.

12 For the nose, create a rounded triangle shape out of the cereal mixture. Attach the nose to the center of the face.

13 For the bridge, create a Y shape out of the cereal mixture. (The bridge will make the eyes look more indented and set into the face.) Attach the bridge to the face just above the nose.

14 **Make the ears:** Sculpt and carve cereal mixture into two ear shapes, working with them at the same time to ensure they're symmetrical. Do not attach the ears to the head just yet.

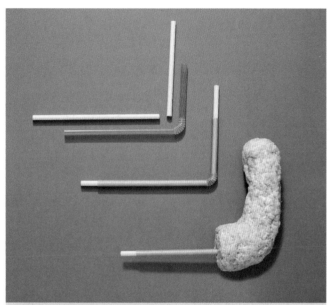

16 Mold the remaining cereal mixture around the straw and lollipop sticks, leaving about 3 inches of lollipop stick uncovered on the long end. Make this arm roughly the same size as the right arm, and make the paw end slightly rounded. Use a small serrated knife to trim the arm and resculpt it around the straw until you are happy with the shape. Place the finished arm on an 8-inch cake board.

17 Using uncolored buttercream, crumb coat the cakes and puffed rice parts—the body, head, both ears, and left arm. Chill for 20 to 30 minutes, until the crumb coat is firm to the touch.

18 Retrieve both cakes, the ears, and the left arm from the fridge. Apply another layer of uncolored buttercream to everything—head, body, ears, left arm—as smoothly as possible. For the left arm, try to create a smooth surface without using too much buttercream. Chill everything for 20 to 30 minutes, until the buttercream is firm to the touch.

19 **Cover the body with fondant:**
With a fabric measuring tape, measure the body from the base of one side, up and over to the base of the other. Dust the work surface with confectioners' sugar and use a wooden rolling pin to roll out a circle of white fondant ⅛ inch thick and a little larger than your measurement. Set a French rolling pin in the center of the fondant and fold one end up over it. Try not to handle the fondant too much. Pick up the pin, then quickly and carefully drape the fondant over the cake front to back. Because there are quite a few grooves, it's easier to smooth with your fingertips, but you can use a fondant smoother for the top and back.

20 Repeat this process to cover the head.

21 **Cover the left arm and ears:** Roll out a little piece of white fondant large enough to cover the whole arm. Drape it over one side and smooth it onto the arm. Flip the arm over, gather the excess fondant, and trim it at the back with a paring knife, creating a seam that's as clean as possible. Roll out two little pieces of white fondant, drape them over the ears, smooth with your fingertips, and cut away the excess at the base.

22 **Insert dowels into the body:** Place a 1½-inch circle cutter on top of the body to use as a guide and insert one unsharpened dowel straight down and all the way into the body. Mark the dowel with a pencil where it is flush with the cake, then remove it from the cake and cut four lengths of dowel to that size (from two unsharpened dowels). Insert them around the circle cutter at the 12, 3, 6, and 9 o'clock positions.

23 **Attach the head to the body:** Measure the height of the body plus three-quarters of the way up the head. Trim the remaining dowel to that measurement, then sharpen both ends. Insert the dowel down through the middle of the body and bang it in gently with a hammer so that it goes right into the cake drum (offering the most support). Apply a few dabs of royal icing between the dowels and not too close to the edge of the body. Gently pick up the head on its 3-inch cake board, making sure there is no tape on the bottom of the board. Make sure the face is lined up with the front of the body. Line up the pilot hole with the pointed dowel and slide the head over the dowel to meet the body. If the head does not easily slide down the dowel, very gently press down with the tips of your fingers, being careful not to leave any marks on the fondant.

24 **Attach the ears:** Position the ears at the top of the head, leaving 1 inch between them and making sure they are symmetrically placed on each side. If needed, trim the bases to fit the curve of the head. Glue the ears down with royal icing. If you feel they are not secure enough, you can use lollipop sticks or toothpicks to attach them. At the base of each ear, brush on a little royal icing to close up any seams.

If you're not happy with the puffed rice ears, you can try again using white gum paste instead of cereal mixture—see the Piggy Bank cake (page 157, step 21) for ear instructions.

25 **Make the cat's collar:** Measure the circumference of the cat's neck and roll out a band of light purple fondant ¼ inch thick, a little longer than that measurement, and about 1 inch wide. Cut it into a ½-inch-wide band using a ruler and a sharp knife. Wrap this around the neck of the cat, using a bit of piping gel on the back to attach it. Cut a clean seam where the ends overlap—make sure this is on the back of the cake.

Once your start using the veining tool you can't reverse it, so using the circle cutter first to help mark is much like using a pencil to sketch.

26 **Accentuate the cat's facial features:** Place a 2-inch oval cutter just beside the nose bridge and make a slight marking for the inner corner of each eye socket where you will indent with a veining tool. Accentuate the marks with the veining tool, starting lightly and then deepening them, running up along each side of the nose to the starting point of the brow.

27 Make all the details before you attach them. First, make the teal details: For the cat's bib, measure from the bottom of the collar and down the belly of the cat, then across the chest of the cat. On a nonstick mat or board, using a small nonstick rolling pin, roll out some of the teal fondant and cut out a crest shape with a scooped top (to fit the neck). Don't worry about making it perfect; you can adjust it when you put it on the cat.

28 **Make the cat's eyes:** Roll out more teal fondant as thin as possible and cut out two eyes. You can cut them by hand, creating a template based on your own lucky cat. I tend to use my kitchen tools in creative ways; here I used a leaf cutter. (The pupils will be made with black fondant later.)

29 **Make the pink details:** Roll out all the pink fondant until 1/16 inch thick. Cut two bands 1/4 inch wide and long enough to run along the sides of the teal bib.

30 For the cat's fingernails and toenails, use a #8 round piping tip to cut out 16 pink circles.

31 For the inside of the cat's ears, use a 2-inch oval cutter to cut pink ovals. (Because your cat's ears might be a different size from mine, you may need to use another size cutter.)

Thank goodness Jeremy, our photographer, used to be an English teacher in Japan and was able to help me out with my characters!

32 For the cat's nose and mouth, roll pink fondant into a little ball between your hands, then model it into a rounded and pointed triangle, like a little bunny nose. For the mouth, roll out a little cord of pink fondant; pinch it up in the center and curve the ends to create a cupid's bow shape. It's helpful to do this beside the nose so that it's in proportion.

33 **Make the yellow gum paste details:** To make the coin, roll out the yellow gum paste on the nonstick mat with the nonstick pin until 1/2 inch thick. Cut out an oval using a 3-inch oval cutter; it's helpful to grease the sides of your oval cutter with a bit of vegetable shortening, since you're cutting through a thick piece of gum paste. Press a #2 strip cutter into the gum paste to create the horizontal lines on it.

34 For the bell, roll a small ball of yellow gum paste between your hands. Use the back of a knife to create the slit in the bell, then use a pointed sculpting tool to indent at each end of the slit.

35 **Make the black details:** Roll out the black fondant as thin as possible. On the coin, I chose to spell out the word *cake* in Japanese, but you can write whatever you want, such as the name of the person you're making the cake for. I made my characters using an "I" letter cutter: I cut out seven letters and positioned them to spell "cake."

36 For the pupils, cut out two circles using an #807 round piping tip.

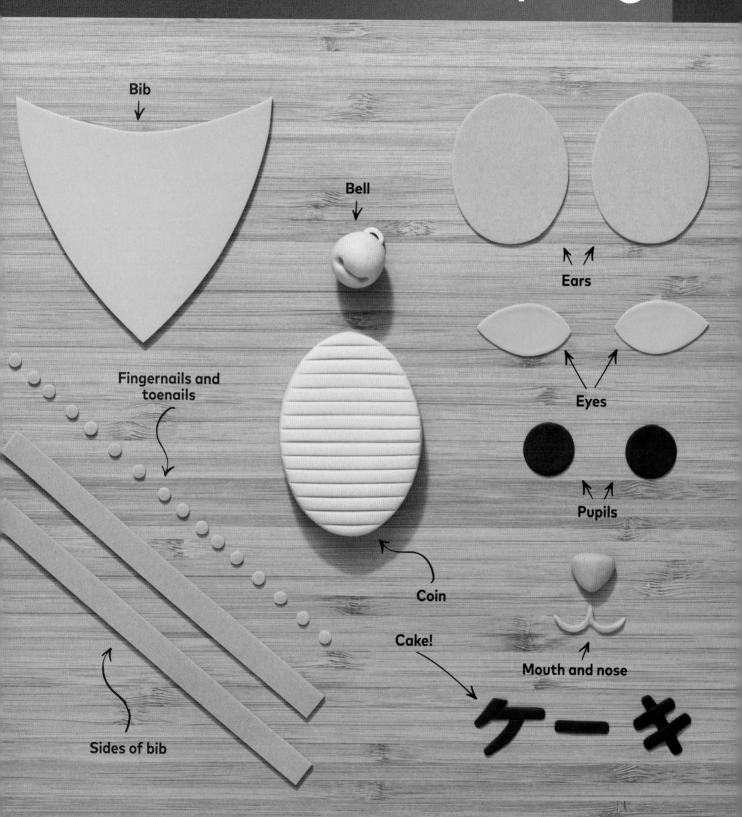

Bib

Bell

Ears

Eyes

Fingernails and toenails

Pupils

Coin

Cake!

Mouth and nose

Sides of bib

ケーキ

37 **Now attach all the details:** Brush a little piping gel on the back of the teal bib and position it under the collar. With a paring knife, cut it to fit—you may need to round out the neck area. The arm will interrupt the bib, so cut around it while the bib is on the body. Brush piping gel on the back of the pink bands, and add them alongside the bib, trimming as necessary.

38 Attach four nails to each paw, spaced evenly, by brushing piping gel on the back of the small pink circles. Don't forget to add them to the left arm, which will be added at the very end.

39 Apply piping gel to the back of the nose and attach it to the part of the cat's face that is slightly protruding. Before adding the cupid's bow, use a 1½-inch circle cutter to make a slight half-circle indent under the nose, leaving enough space for the cupid's bow. Apply piping gel to the back of the cupid's bow and attach it to the cake.

40 For the inner ears, brush piping gel on the backs of the pink ovals and attach them to the ears, trimming the ovals where they meet the head.

41 Brush piping gel on the backs of the black pupils and attach them to the teal eyes, making sure they are even and centered. Brush piping gel on the backs of the teal eyes and attach them to the face.

42 To create the outline of the eyes and the eyelashes, knead the black fondant with a bit of vegetable shortening to soften it. Shape it into a cord and feed it into a clay extruder using the smallest round faceplate. Extrude several thin cords of black fondant to use for small details. To begin, with a thin paintbrush, brush a line of piping gel around the eyes and apply the cords incrementally: Start with the bottom of the eye and trim the cord. Next, make the top of the eye with an eyelash at the end; trim the cord. Add another eyelash and trim. Repeat with the other eye.

43 For the whiskers, use an oval cutter to make a slight indent that runs from the side of the mouth up to the brow line. Attach a cord of black fondant to each side of the face that follows the indent. Using shorter cords, add two more whiskers of varying lengths above the main whiskers and one below on each side.

44 To make fingers and toes, cut another cord of black fondant into 12 short lengths. Attach them with piping gel to the hands and feet between the pink dots to separate out fingers and toes.

45 Add catching light to each eye: Roll out a small piece of white fondant as thin as possible. Using a #2 piping tip, cut out two little circles. Glue them to the pupils with piping gel.

46 Make the flowers: Roll out purple, green, and yellow gum paste. Using a five-petal rose cutter, cut out five purple flowers. Cut a little V out of each petal with a small triangle cutter or the tip of your paring knife. Once you're happy with the flowers, use piping gel to attach one to each elbow and one to each knee. For the flower that goes on the top of the cat's head, glue a little ball of purple gum paste behind it to prop it up before attaching it. Create the center of each flower by cutting out small circles of yellow gum paste using a #12 piping tip, and then attach them to the flowers with piping gel. Finally, use a small teardrop cutter or leaf cutter (or cut them by hand with a paring knife) to cut out 15 leaves from the green gum paste (three leaves per flower). Attach them with piping gel.

47 Paint the gold details: Brush the coin and bell all over with a thin layer of shortening, making sure to get into all the crevices. With a dry paintbrush, brush on gold luster dust.

48 While you have your luster dust handy, mix it with a few drops of clear food-grade alcohol until you get a paint-like consistency, then paint a pattern onto the teal bib. I chose to paint simple freehand polka dots and a thin line between the teal and the pink. Allow to dry.

49 Before you attach the coin to the cake, you need to add some more details to it. Make sure to wipe your hands frequently so you don't get luster dust on the fondant. Roll out some of the black fondant into a band that is wider than the thickness of the coin; cut it to the exact thickness of the coin and wrap it around the sides of the coin, attaching it with piping gel. Very carefully attach the characters using piping gel.

50 Hold the coin against the body. I used an oval cutter to trim away a little of the top of the coin to fit the hand and a sharp paring knife to cut a little off the bottom. Attach the coin to the cake with piping gel, making sure that it's snug up against the cake, and carefully trim away the bib so it looks like it's lying underneath the coin.

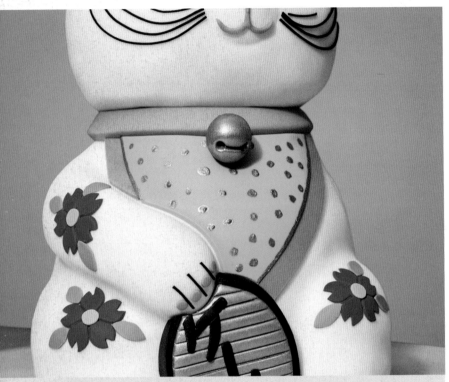

53 **Attach left arm:** Insert two lollipop sticks into the base of the arm, above and below the existing lollipop stick. Insert a lollipop stick into the side of the hand where it will touch the head and add some royal icing to the point where it will stick into the head. Add some royal icing to the center of the arm socket. Now stick the base of the arm into the socket and the hand to the side of the head. With a damp paintbrush, brush away any excess royal icing that oozes out. Hold the arm in place for a few minutes or prop it with something to keep it secure until the royal icing hardens. Now you get to eat this cake! Aren't you lucky?

51 Dab a bit of piping gel on the back of the bell and stick a piece of spaghetti into it, then attach the bell like it's hanging down from the center of the collar.

52 Impress a circle indent on the left side of the cake using a cutter that will fit over the arm. Extrude softened white fondant with the largest round faceplate. Use piping gel to attach the extruded fondant in a circle along the indent. Make sure the seam is at the back so it will be hidden by the arm. This is now an arm socket!

Cake by Numbers
Scaling Guide

Many of these one-of-a-kind cakes require more than one batch of batter or not quite so much buttercream to reach the highest heights. Figuring out the math of how to increase or decrease a recipe can be tricky, though, so here are the scaled ingredient amounts if you need to make more than one recipe, or if you only need to make a half-batch. Most home stand mixers can handle 1½ recipes' worth of batter; if you need to make more than that, you might want to mix in batches. Remember to always carefully follow the instructions for mixing and baking. Now, cake it away!

Ⓒ Yo's Ultimate Chocolate Cake

	1 recipe	1½ recipes	2 recipes
all-purpose flour	2¾ cups	4 cups + 2 tbsp	5½ cups
baking powder	2 teaspoons	1 tablespoon	4 teaspoons
baking soda	1½ teaspoons	2¼ teaspoons	1 tablespoon
table salt	1 teaspoon	1½ teaspoons	2 teaspoons
cocoa powder	1 cup	1½ cups	2 cups
boiling water	2 cups	3 cups	4 cups
unsalted butter	1 cup (2 sticks)	1½ cups (3 sticks)	2 cups (4 sticks)
sugar	2½ cups	3¾ cups	5 cups
large eggs	4	6	8

Ⓥ Yo's Ultimate Vanilla Cake

	1 recipe	1½ recipes	2 recipes
all-purpose flour	2½ cups	3¾ cups	5 cups
baking powder	2½ teaspoons	3¾ teaspoons	5 teaspoons
table salt	½ teaspoon	¾ teaspoon	1 teaspoon
unsalted butter	1 cup (2 sticks)	1½ cups (3 sticks)	2 cups (4 sticks)
sugar	2 cups	3 cups	4 cups
pure vanilla extract	1 teaspoon	1½ teaspoons	2 teaspoons
large eggs	4	6	8
whole milk	1 cup	1½ cups	2 cups

Ⓟ Yo's Pink Velvet Cake

	1 recipe	1½ recipes	2 recipes
all-purpose flour	4 cups	6 cups	8 cups
table salt	2 teaspoons	1 tablespoon	4 teaspoons
unsalted butter	1 cup (2 sticks)	1½ cups (3 sticks)	2 cups (4 sticks)
vegetable oil	⅓ cup	½ cup	⅔ cup
sugar	3 cups	4½ cups	6 cups
pure vanilla extract	1½ teaspoons	2¼ teaspoons	1 tablespoon
large eggs	4	6	8
rose food coloring	1 tablespoon	1½ tablespoons	2 tablespoons
red food coloring	½ teaspoon	¾ teaspoon	1 teaspoon
buttermilk	2 cups	3 cups	4 cups
baking soda	2 teaspoons	1 tablespoon	4 teaspoons
cider vinegar	2 teaspoons	1 tablespoon	4 teaspoons

Yo's Coconut Cake

	1 recipe	1½ recipes	2 recipes
all-purpose flour	3 cups	4½ cups	6 cups
baking power	1 tablespoon	4½ teaspoons	2 tablespoons
sweetened desiccated coconut	1 cup	1½ cups	2 cups
salted butter	1 cup (2 sticks)	1½ cups (3 sticks)	2 cups (4 sticks)
sugar	2 cups	3 cups	4 cups
pure vanilla extract	2 teaspoons	1 tablespoon	4 teaspoons
large egg whites	4	6	8
large whole eggs	4	6	8
unsweetened coconut milk	2⅓ cups	3½ cups	4⅔ cups

Yo's Italian Meringue Buttercream

	½ recipe	1 recipe
sugar	¾ cup + 2 tbsp	1¾ cups
water	¼ cup	½ cup
large egg whites	4	8
unsalted butter	1 cup (2 sticks)	2 cups (4 sticks)
pure vanilla extract	½ teaspoon	1 teaspoon

Yo's Chocolate Swiss Meringue Buttercream

	½ recipe	1 recipe
dark chocolate	9 ounces	18 ounces
sugar	½ cup	1 cup
table salt	⅛ teaspoon	¼ teaspoon
cream of tartar	pinch	⅛ teaspon
large egg whites	2	4

Yo's Dark Chocolate Ganache

	½ recipe	1 recipe	1½ recipes	2 recipes
dark chocolate (72%)	8 ounces	1 pound	1½ pounds	2 pounds
whipping cream	1 cup	2 cups	2¾ cups	3¾ cups

Conversion Charts

Oven temperature equivalents

250°F = 120°C

275°F = 135°C

300°F = 150°C

325°F = 160°C

350°F = 180°C

375°F = 190°C

400°F = 200°C

425°F = 220°C

450°F = 230°C

475°F = 240°C

500°F = 260°C

Measurement equivalents

Measurements should always be level unless directed otherwise.

⅛ teaspoon = 0.5 mL

¼ teaspoon = 1 mL

½ teaspoon = 2 mL

1 teaspoon = 5 mL

1 tablespoon = 3 teaspoons = ½ fluid ounce = 15 mL

2 tablespoons = ⅛ cup = 1 fluid ounce = 30 mL

4 tablespoons = ¼ cup = 2 fluid ounces = 60 mL

5⅓ tablespoons = ⅓ cup = 3 fluid ounces = 80 mL

8 tablespoons = ½ cup = 4 fluid ounces = 120 mL

10⅔ tablespoons = ⅔ cup = 5 fluid ounces = 160 mL

12 tablespoons = ¾ cup = 6 fluid ounces = 180 mL

16 tablespoons = 1 cup = 8 fluid ounces = 240 mL

Shout-Outs to the Dream Team

To my husband, David—Thank you for all you have done for me and continue to do for me. Thank you for being my partner, my friend, and for holding my hand through our journey. I love you always, and I could not have done this without you.

To my son—You are the love of my life. I was forever changed the moment I met you. You continue to make me proud every day. I thank you for the perspective you have given me, which allows me to see life through your eyes. I love you more than I can say.

To Connie Contardi—How lucky I am to have worked on this book with you! I have enjoyed this process tremendously, and you are a major part of that. To be clear ;) your patience, eternal optimism, and unwavering commitment to all you do is beyond admirable. I love you.

To Jocelyn Mercer—My cutthroat butterfly. I am always inspired by your strength, support, and guidance. You bring so much more to our YouTube channel than giggles behind a camera. You come with your A game, ambition, and positive energy every single day. But I do love the giggles ... and the green juice. I love you.

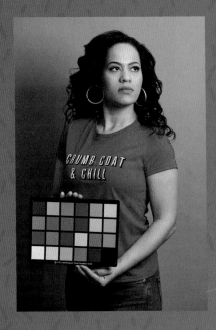

To Jeremy Kohm—This book wouldn't have been possible without your dedication, talent, sacrifice, and, of course, your tolerance of our inside jokes. Quite frankly, you're, like, totally amazing!

To Orhan Sümen—Our Turkish Prince, graphics guru (ha!), and calm, patient anchor on *How To Cake It! You* are so loved by us all. Thank you.

To Larissa Contardi—Your smile, energy, and dedication are a gift. We appreciate all you do for the *How To Cake It* community, and for us.

To Chet Tilokan—The original, one and only, never to be replaced. We were lucky to get "27-year-old Chet"—a game changer! We can't put into words our love and appreciation for you. 99 Problems but a Cake Ain't One. Coming soon.

To Tenille Villebrun, Sasha Hill, Ammie Matte, Rachel Kellogg, Hailey Coleman, and Katelyn Cursio—You are all Wonder Women, and such important parts of *How To Cake It*—we love you. Tenille, your support from the beginning will never be forgotten—you edited the very first episodes of *HTCI* and helped us get this baby off the ground. Sasha, you are such a wise, patient, and beautiful person and became an extra light on our set. Ammie, your empathy and ability to know exactly what we were thinking made working with you a dream. Rachel, your positivity, hard work, and integrity ignited a cascade of goodness we can't thank you enough for. Hailey, you were a KEY part of our launch, and your incredible insight and enthusiasm have been invaluable. Katelyn, you truly embody the definition of work ethic—you are consistently willing to jump in, do what needs to be done, and offer support. Throughout life you will be rewarded for this in more ways than you can imagine.

To our incredible e-commerce team—Your hard work, willingness to grow, and the positive way you support our amazing community is so appreciated!

To Ryan Pastorek—The secret is out: the real reason we brought you on is because we loved your nature photography! Ha! Thank you for being our knight on an ever-changing battlefield, and for standing up for our best interests.

To Rick Matthews—Your Instagram feed gives us FOMO, but other than that you're a gem. You have been such a positive support from the beginning—we are SO glad you found us at YouTube FanFest. Let's keep having fun. Thank you to the whole Kin Community for everything.

To Pizzaville and the Contardi family—You have been instrumental in the growth of How To Cake It and a valuable resource when it comes to building our brand. Oh, and the delicious pizza now and then has been pretty awesome, too. :)

To Sonali, Graham, and everyone at YouTube—If YouTube didn't exist, I'd still be making cakes for one client at a time. Now millions of people can enjoy them as much as I do. We can't thank you enough. Sonali, you'll always be our #DayOne. Graham, your guidance is proving invaluable. And **Susan**, you told us to dream big, and we hope you're still doing the same. ;)

To Kate Cassaday, Cassie Jones, and everyone at HarperCollins—What a ride this has been! Thank you for being on it with us and seeing the potential for a book in what we built. We made it! Didn't we tell you these cakes were nothing to mess with? :) And a special thank you to Gareth Lind for making this book look so great on such a tight deadline.

To Michelle Zubrinich—Your extra touch on this book has really made it sparkle. Thank you.

To Liana Krissoff—I've never worked with an editor before, but if this is what it's like, it's amazing! Your steady support and guidance have made all the difference. We are all grateful for the chain of events that brought us together.

To Jenia O'Connor, Vanessa Garland, and Marie-Eve Tremblay—Thank you for helping me to look my best.

To my mother, Cynthia—What can I say about the woman who has always supported me and let me be me? I can only hope to be that kind of mother to my son. I love you.

To my sister Lisa—I hope all the grammar in this book is correct, because if it's not, I know you'll point it out to me! :) Thank you for being great at all the things I'm not. I love you.

To Bianca—Since our first day in art class (26 years ago!!!) I've always been inspired by your creativity. I can't tell you how happy I am that we were able to collaborate on some of the photos in this book. I love you.

To Suad—You are the most fiery, ambitious, fearless woman I have ever met. I stick by your side always hoping that some of it will rub off. ;) I adore you.

To Sally and Patricia—Great friends are like stars: you don't always see them, but you know they are there. You are my oldest and dearest friends and will always have a place in my life.

To my son's guncles, Caspar and Derek—You came into my life at the perfect time and brought a completely new perspective. We have been through so much together—the shortest phone call with either of you will have me in stitches and brighten my day. #FamJam

To my husband's amazing family, which has become my family—Your love and support mean the world. David, P, and I couldn't have done this without you.

We would collectively like to thank our entire support group of family, friends, and significant others—Every single one of you makes us better versions of ourselves, believes in our work, and puts up with the long hours, missed events, and exhaustion. Because you hold us up, we are free to fly!

Replicake

Rep.li.cake ('repl,kāke). Verb. *The activity of watching a How To Cake It video and then recreating the cake featured in it, often putting your own unique spin on it. The replicaked cake does not need to be perfect or even close to perfect. The most important thing is that you caked it, had fun in the process, and enjoyed the sweet results with others afterwards. Bonus points for sharing with the How To Cake It community on social media!*

I am so grateful for each and every one of you who watches me cake my dreams on YouTube every Tuesday. I appreciate every subscriber and every view, but I especially love seeing you dive into the fun yourself. *How To Cake It* is more than just a show—it's an invitation to be inspired and get creative in your kitchen, in your community, and beyond. It makes my heart so happy to see the amazing creations my YoYos from all around the world make and share, so please keep on watching, replicaking, and, of course, sharing!

Xo Yo

Sir Squeeze Cinco De Mayo

Breyonna Jones, 24
Mareitta, Georgia, USA

Baker. "I started baking alongside my mom when I was a little girl! I had always made cakes for fun. When I had my baby in 2016, I wanted to stay at home with him, and that's when I decided to start Sugar Shack so I could bake and decorate cakes full time!"

Nachos

Avery Heeringa, 15
Saint Paul, Minnesota, USA

SuperYOYO. "I have been baking for about two years now. I love HTCI because it makes me happy when I watch. My fave vid is the S'Moreo Cake!"

Alba Trevisiol, 56
Miami, Florida, USA

Architect. "Baking has brought me great joy, and has brought me and my family closer."

Andrea Sullivan, 38
Brampton, Ontario, Canada

Self-taught cake artist. "My favorite HTCI video would have to be Yo's Giant Cupcake. That's right up my alley!"

Beach Bag

Donut/ Coffee

Unicorn Popcorn

Cinthia Itzel Michel, 26
Midland, Texas, USA

Business owner. "I started baking when I was 10 years old, and always wanted to become a pastry chef."

Breakfast in Bed

Carlos Ferreira Filho, 22
Brazil

Baker. "I started working at the bakery about three years ago. Unicorn Cornucopia Cake is my fave HTCI cake."

**Brandi Margaret Lindoe, 22
Clem, South Carolina, USA**

Bakery owner. "I started baking
when I was 15 years old. At 21, I
opened a bake shop called Clemson
Confectioneries. I absolutely love
How To Cake It! Yolanda simplifies
every cake in such a beautiful and
graceful way!"

**Gabriela Vaughan Flatt, 27
Chandler, Arizona, USA**

Special education teacher. "I love to
bake and decorate cakes and desserts
for friends and family. I have an amazing
husband who has supported me and all
of my baking, even though it sometimes
takes over the kitchen!"

**Hannah Nguyen, 24
Melbourne, Australia**

Cake decorating teacher. "I began
baking simple cupcakes for students
at the local Charity Tuition Centre,
and every now and then for special
occasions. My fun hobby turned
into a passion, and then eventually
landed me a gig as a cake
decorating teacher."

**Avinesh Wadhwa, 30
Delhi, India**

Catering company owner, "I started
baking eight years ago when I moved
7,500 miles away from Delhi, to Windsor,
Ontario, Canada, to study. Baking
became a passion and was incredibly
therapeutic. Four years ago, I moved back
home and started a catering company."

**Rafia Siddiq, 14
Walnut, California, USA**

"I love watching HTCI because the
videos always make me laugh. My
favorite is the BB-8 cake. I love
how close it looks to BB-8 from
the movie."

**Montana Rae Ferrill, 25
Scarborough, Ontario,
Canada**

Montana developed a passion for
caking after she dropped her mom's
birthday cake and tried her hand at
making a replacement herself.

Box of Chocolates

**Jade Moore, 23
Sydney, Australia**

"I find HTCI incredibly soothing to watch. Yolanda's precision is amazing, and she truly inspires me to be as precise with my own work."

Water-melon

**Samantha Ho, 33
Barcelona, Spain**

"I started baking about two years ago, mostly out of boredom. I wanted to try something new, and I've always loved desserts and sweets. After a few hits and definitely a few misses, I got hooked! My dream is to one day do this full time."

Social Media Icon

**Tabitha Martel, 32
Eureka, California, USA**

SuperYOYO. Tabitha's passion for baking stemmed from watching her grandma ice a lemon cake "as smooth as I've ever seen." Now she loves watching Yo, who makes it easy to learn and understand how to cake.

Vase of Flowers

**Giovanna & Simone Negri
Giovanna is 7
Sao Paulo, Brazil**

SuperYOYOs. Giovanna and her mom, Simone, were two of my very first fans—now we even exchange birthday cards and gifts!

Social Icon

**Sara Fawaz Fattal Ybroudi, 20
Jeddah, Saudi Arabia**

"I started baking in 2015, and it has become my passion. I love HTCI because you make baking fun and easy. I'm grateful for everything I have learned from you. And I love your characters playlists!"

WANT MORE?

Your caking journey doesn't have to end here!

Check out *How To Cake It* on YouTube for dozens more fun and fearless cakes.

Visit howtocakeit.com to buy Sir Squeeze-A-Lot, cake tees, and everything else you need to *cake it away!*

Cake It Your Own!

The finishing details on all of my cakes are always just a suggestion—let your imagination run wild (and share your cake masterpieces with me on social media)! Mix and match cake flavors and customize the decoration—it's your creation! Here are just a few ideas to help get your creative caking juices flowing.

Mix and Match Patterns

- Paint the Purse cake pattern onto a Party Hat cake.

- Try putting the stars from the Party Hat cake on a Sand Pail cake.

- Create a golden Piggy Bank cake instead of a pink one.

- Make a pink (or purple or green or red) bulldozer.

Make It Seasonal

- Use seasonal cookie cutters to make holiday wrapping paper for your Gift Box cake.

- Who doesn't love a candy apple at Halloween? Create a themed Candy Apple cake by adding black and orange candy, and then top it off with a ghoulish bow.

- Change the colors on the Rainbow Grilled Cheese cake to match the season, such as creating green cheese for St. Patrick's Day!

Pick Your Perfect Details

- Make a Black Forest Giant Cake Slice by working with chocolate fondant.

- Why not try silver hardware on your Purse cake, like on the Tool Box cake?

- Substitute the cherry and sprinkles from the Giant Cake Slice for the peak on your Soft Serve Cone cake.

- Take your Purse cake from day to night by adding jewels from the Crown cake.

It's What's Inside That Counts

- Bake up the vanilla tie-dye batter from the Marquee Letters cake for your Lucky Cat cake.

- Use the chocolate sprinkles batter from the Golden Pyramid cake to make a Toolbox cake.

- Make an all-chocolate Soft Serve Cone cake and change up the cone color—why not try pink?

Index

Note: Page references in **bold** indicate photos of finished cakes.

Yolanda Gampp

is a self-taught cake artist who started out baking novelty cakes in her mother's kitchen and is now one of the forces behind *How To Cake It*, a hugely successful, Webby Award–winning YouTube channel and online community of over six million cake enthusiasts from around the world.

Yolanda and her work have been featured on the *Today Show*, and in *BuzzFeed*, *Daily Mail*, and *Cosmopolitan*, while Yolanda has served as a guest judge on popular Food Network shows such as *Cake Wars* and *Sugar Showdown*.

Inspired by her father, who worked as a baker, Yolanda graduated from chef's school and discovered that her true passion was working with sweets. She lives in Toronto, Canada, with her husband (Mr. Cake) and young son.